MILLENNIAL MONEY

MILLENNIAL MONEY

HOW YOUNG INVESTORS CAN BUILD A FORTUNE

PATRICK O'SHAUGHNESSY

palgrave
macmillan

MILLENNIAL MONEY

Copyright © Patrick O'Shaughnessy, 2014.

First published in 2014 by
PALGRAVE MACMILLAN® TRADE
in the United States—a division of St. Martin's Press LLC,
175 Fifth Avenue, New York, NY 10010.

Where this book is distributed in the UK, Europe and the rest of the world,
this is by Palgrave Macmillan, a division of Macmillan Publishers Limited,
registered in England, company number 785998, of Houndmills,
Basingstoke, Hampshire RG21 6XS.

Palgrave® and Macmillan® are registered trademarks in the United States,
the United Kingdom, Europe, and other countries.

ISBN: 978–1–137–27925–5

Library of Congress Cataloging-in-Publication Data

O'Shaughnessy, Patrick.
   Millennial money : how young investors can build a fortune /
Patrick O'Shaughnessy.
      pages cm
   ISBN 978–1–137–27925–5 (hardback)
      1. Finance, Personal. 2. Investments. 3. Securities. I. Title.

HG179.O7787 2014
332.6—dc23   2014005212

A catalogue record of the book is available from the British Library.

Design by Newgen Knowledge Works (P) Ltd., Chennai, India.

First edition: October 2014

10 9 8 7 6 5 4 3 2 1

Printed in the United States of America.

For Lauren, who makes me happy

CONTENTS

Acknowledgments   ix

Disclaimer   xi

Introduction   1

1   The Millennial Edge   11

2   Building Good Financial Karma   31

3   Investing Principles   53

4   Go Global   57

5   Be Different   69

6   The Millennial Money Strategy   91

7   Get Out of Your Own Way   125

8   The Long Game   143

9   The Push and the Pull   163

10 Opportunity Knocks   181

Notes   197

Index   208

ACKNOWLEDGMENTS

Writing this book was as challenging as it was rewarding. My name may be on the cover, but the book was a collaborative effort. The best part about the writing process was working with those I love and respect. To all of you who helped me along the way, I am thankful.

My agent, Wesley Neff, and my editor, Laurie Harting, played a huge role in the book's direction and tone. Thanks to their guidance, what started as a generic investment book morphed into a book targeted at a specific generation—a change that resulted in a much more focused message. I thank them both for recognizing that, because I am a young author, my message is best tailored to young investors. I further thank Laurie for helping me find my voice. This being my first book, the early chapter drafts were rather dull and my writing style rather dry. Laurie helped me realize that just being myself would make this book more entertaining and more interesting. In addition to Laurie, everyone at Palgrave Macmillan was a pleasure to work with. Thank you all for helping to make this book a reality.

My colleagues at O'Shaughnessy Asset Management have been very supportive as well. I owe a special thanks to Travis Fairchild, Ash Viswanathan, Chris Meredith, and Scott Bartone. Travis read the entire book and helped me edit the final chapters—if there was a superhero whose power was attention to detail, it would be Travis. Scott read the book's most important sections and offered very helpful feedback. Ash and Chris both helped me hone the investing strategy I recommend in chapter 6.

I'd also like to thank a group of writers whose books, articles, and essays made me want to become a writer. David Mitchell, Michael Pollan, Laura Hillenbrand, Cormac McCarthy, Isaac Asimov, Julian Barnes, Aldous Huxley, Alan Watts, Will and Ariel Durant, Eknath Easwaran, Jiddu Krishnamurti, and Joseph Campbell all changed my outlook on writing and on life. I haven't matched their standard, but I am deeply appreciative to each for their inspiration.

I owe the most gratitude to my family. My father's endless curiosity inspired my own interest in investing, and his guidance and mentorship throughout this process has been invaluable. My mother's eye for quality—along with the many rounds of edits she helped me complete—made this final version possible. I also owe a special thanks to my sister Kate. Her pointed and insightful feedback on each chapter and her many creative suggestions made this a much better book. To my sister Lael: thanks for supplying me with a constant stream of great music to keep me going.

Finally, I could not have completed this project without my beautiful wife Lauren and newborn son Pierce. Lauren tolerated my many weekends at the keyboard, contemplative space-staring episodes, and frustrated bouts of writers block—all while pregnant. As with all things in my life, she was my rock, my fuel, and my inspiration. She gave me the confidence to write my first book, and supported me with love and humor. To my new son Pierce: when you read this someday, you should know that your impending arrival was useful in two important ways. First, your due date set a hard deadline for me to complete the book, which might have taken me years otherwise. Second, and more importantly, knowing that you were on your way made me want to write something that would make you proud of your dad someday. I hope I have delivered.

DISCLAIMER

All information in this book is the property of O'Shaughnessy or the information providers and is protected by copyright and intellectual property laws. You may not reproduce, retransmit, disseminate, sell, publish, broadcast, or circulate the information or material in this book without the express written consent of O'Shaughnessy or the other information providers herein. This book does not constitute investment advice from O'Shaughnessy, his publisher, affiliates, or O'Shaughnessy Asset Management LLC.

This book contains statements and statistics that have been obtained from sources believed to be reliable but are not guaranteed as to accuracy or completeness. Neither O'Shaughnessy nor the information providers can guarantee the accuracy, completeness, or timeliness of any of the information in the book, including, but not limited to information originating with O'Shaughnessy, licensed by O'Shaughnessy from information providers, or gathered by O'Shaughnessy from publicly available sources. There may be omissions or inaccuracies in the information contained in the book. Neither O'Shaughnessy, the publisher, nor any of the information providers shall have any liability, contingent or otherwise, for the accuracy, completeness, or timeliness of the information or for any decision made or action taken by you in reliance upon the information in this book. Neither O'Shaughnessy, the publisher, nor the information providers make any representations about the suitability of the information contained in the book and all such information is provided "as is" without warranty of any kind.

INTRODUCTION

This book explores one of youth's greatest advantages: the chance to build a fortune by making early investments in the stock market. Unfortunately, this is an advantage that is too often wasted on the young. We tend to start investing too late, and in so doing miss our once-in-a-lifetime chance to build significant personal wealth. While many miss out on this chance, you don't have to. *Millennial Money* explores every facet of your opportunity. It describes why youth trumps everything in investing, how your investments will protect you from obstacles in the future, and what you need to do to transform your small early investments into large sums. The task is surprisingly straightforward—all you need to do is start young and choose investments that will grow your money at the most impressive rate. But with so many investment options out there—and so many ways to make mistakes—it is important to make smart decisions early on. This book will show you why you should start investing now, show you how to build a winning portfolio, and teach you to become a successful investor.

* * *

It's funny that we spend so many hours each week working hard to earn money and build our careers, but then spend very little time thinking about how to put our money to good use. This is a shame, because your young money—even in modest amounts—has tremendous potential. It is up to you to make that potential a reality. Money's potential fades with time, so there is no time like the present to get started. One dollar invested today can easily be worth $15 in forty years; but if you wait ten more years to get started, the same dollar might only grow to $7.50. Imagine how different your lifestyle would be in your later years with twice the amount of money in the bank.

Think of yourself as a business. You earn and you spend, just like any business. A good business spends less than it earns in sales, so that it produces profits. The fastest growing businesses are ones that take those profits and reinvest in themselves in order to grow. You should mimic this business plan. If you spend everything you earn, then you won't grow. Instead, you should spend less than you earn and reinvest those personal profits for future growth. The success of this "personal" business plan depends on two things: how much you save and what you do with your savings. Unfortunately, Americans are moving in the wrong direction on both counts.

The savings rate—which is the best way to measure our "personal profit margin"—has been falling for decades. In the 1970s, Americans saved about 12 percent of their income. The savings rate has fallen ever since, all the way to 4.2 percent in November 2013. Where you put your savings is key, and the stock market is the best way to make your money grow, but investors in general—and millennials specifically—have grown skeptical of the market. Millennials worry about the future, but our experiences have left us leery of risky investments. A survey conducted in 2013 found that our generation's top concern was having enough money for retirement: 73 percent of millennial respondents said that they were "worried," "somewhat worried," or "very worried" about a secure retirement.[1] But a second survey found that 52 percent of millennials were "not very confident" or "not confident at all" that the stock market was a good place to invest for retirement.[2] Clearly, the two market crashes that we've lived through, in 2000 and 2008, have both made a lasting impression on our opinions about stocks.

These two trends need reversing. You should invest as high a percentage of your income as possible, and you should invest in the global stock market rather than in "low-risk" alternatives like cash or bonds.

As I will explore, you should invest in the stock market for two reasons.

First, you should invest so that you can passively participate in business growth around the world, which has always advanced at an impressive rate—so impressive that stocks have always trumped all alternatives. Think of the companies that produce your favorite products or offer the best services—the shareholders of those companies have reaped huge rewards. Think of one such product: the iPod. In October 2001, the cost of a shiny new, first generation iPod was $500. At the time, the same $500 would have bought you 64 shares of Apple stock. The 2001 iPod has been rendered obsolete ten times over, but the 64 shares are now worth $32,308. Investing is better than spending. When you own shares of a company, you have thousands of people working for you; you get to ride the wave of global innovation and growth. The sea can be choppy at times, but over the long term you will be rewarded handsomely for participating in the global market.

Second, you should invest to protect yourself from a wide range of risks in the future—like income inequality, rising debt, and an aging population. Other options, like cash and bonds, *will not* offer you the same protection. This may strike you as backward—many people dislike stocks because they think that they are too risky. "Risk" is the slippery pig of the investing world, with countless definitions. Unfortunately, most definitions of risk are focused on the short term. They measure how much an investment bounces around over months or a year. Evaluated this way, stocks are indeed risky. But risk should be a long-term measure. *Real* risk is the chance that (1) you *won't* achieve your financial goals and the dreams associated with those goals and (2) that you *won't* be able to support yourself (and your loved ones) comfortably later in life. If you define risk as I do, then stocks become the safest place for your money. The investing rules I propose in *Millennial Money* help eliminate these real risks.

The main reason I wrote this book was to highlight the unique chance for the largest generation in history to succeed where past generations have failed. But I wouldn't have written a book about investing if the topic weren't also a ton of fun to explore. In college, I studied philosophy—not finance—so my interest in the stock market was first sparked by investor behavior—not math. The market is a projection of the collective human psyche—all our hopes and fears are projected onto market prices. In this way, the market is one big human psychology experiment, but it is a twisted one because—as in Alice's Wonderland—everything up is down and everything down is up. All the skills we have accumulated as a species through millennia of natural selection are useless in the stock market. If something feels good to you, it'll likely be bad for your portfolio; and if something seems terrifying, it is probably an opportunity in a very convincing disguise. We love safety, but places for your money that seem safe are often dangerous. We generally abhor risks and are skeptical of stocks, but only by investing in stocks can you build a fortune.

As I will explore, successful investing is often contrarian and counterintuitive. If you go against the crowd, buck the current trends, and ignore your emotions, you will succeed. The rules I suggest will help you excel in this topsy-turvy world. Once you get your portfolio started, there are three specific investor tendencies that you'll want to avoid, which I will explain in detail.

1. Investors tend to favor companies in their home country. Americans prefer Coca-Cola to Suntory (a Japanese drinks company) because they are more familiar with Coca-Cola. They can read about Coca-Cola in the newspaper, see the company's CEO on TV, and get a Coke in any vending machine. Investors fear the unknown, so they invest their money locally and ignore great international companies. You should do the opposite by building a global portfolio.

2. More and more investors are conformists who are opting out of the market battlefield, resigning themselves to earning a return that matches the entire market but never exceeds it. You should do the opposite, using the strategies I suggest to build a unique portfolio. Investing in the overall stock market isn't a bad thing— it's still better than non-stock options—but if you do, you'll miss the opportunity to earn even better returns in the long run.

3. Investors let their emotions cloud their judgment. They think short term, move in and out of the market at exactly the wrong times, and succumb to greed and fear. In short, they buy high and sell low. You should do the opposite by mastering your emotions and making your investment plan automatic.

The methods, strategies, and tools for implementing this plan were once available only to the privileged few. Now, they are available to everyone, easy to use, and cheap to implement. In addition to having youth on your side, this easy access to markets gives you a leg up on previous generations.

The book is laid out as follows. Chapters 1 and 2 set the stage and the stakes for millennial investors, explaining our advantages and our challenges. Chapter 1 describes why being young is the biggest investing edge and why stocks are the only choice for young investors in the modern market environment. Chapter 2 looks ahead to several obstacles that lay in our path—including demographic trends and rising debt—and shows why building a stock portfolio will allow you to overcome these obstacles with ease. Chapter 3 introduces three simple principles to follow when investing in the stock market: *go global, be different, and get out of your own way.* These principles are defined in detail in chapters 4 through 9. Chapter 4 discusses why investors tend to buy stocks in their home country but should instead build a global portfolio. Chapters 5 and 6 assess different strategies for investing in the stock market, ranging from basic index funds that hold every meaningful company in the world, to small concentrated portfolios that can beat the market. Chapters 7, 8, and 9 explain why the most important variable in any investing strategy is *you.* These three chapters explore the behavioral traps you will encounter in the years to come, and give you ways to avoid them. Chapter 10 reviews the lessons from the book and provides a variety of resources for putting the plan into action.

If you already invest a chunk of your earnings, great—this book will still help you improve your investing strategy. If you haven't started investing, this book will explain why every year you spend procrastinating is a precious opportunity wasted; nothing in investing is as important as *when* you start. Either way, you will be well equipped to tackle the daunting investing world.

Here is what you will learn reading *Millennial Money*:

- Why youth is your number one edge, and why millennials today have more advantages than any other group in history.
- Why you should start investing now, or invest more than you already do.

- Why you should make most or all of your investments in the *global* stock market.
- How investments in the stock market will protect you from political and economic roadblocks in the future.
- How building a unique portfolio will lead to outstanding market-beating returns. Because of the power of compounding returns—which I explore in chapter 1—every dollar you save today can grow to $15 if you invest in the overall stock market, but if you commit to being different, using strategies like those presented in chapters 5 and 6, then every dollar you save today could be worth more than $90 when you retire.
- Why the best way to be different is to own solid businesses trading at cheap prices that the market is *just* starting to notice.
- Why your behavior is as important as any other variable to achieve investment success, and how you can avoid the most common behavioral pitfalls.

Call to Action

When I was doing the initial research for this book, I delved deep into the history of money itself, hoping to find threads from the past that could inform our decisions for the future. At the same time, I discovered the author Joseph Campbell, whose "hero's journey" could have been written about several legendary investors.

What I learned was that we admire heroes—real and imaginary—because they strive for greatness by taking risks in the face of an uncertain future. Great heroes become symbols that are imbued with meanings that reflect the tests that they have faced—and conquered—as they pursued their reward. Wading through the history of money, I found that the original sign for the US dollar is one such symbol. Like America itself, it was born of heroism and risk, and hidden in its story is a message for young investors.

The story goes like this. The most common Spanish coin used in the British colonies in 1776 was known as the "pillar dollar," named for the twin pillars on its obverse side. This coin had its roots in the myth of Hercules and his twelve seemingly impossible labors—his Herculean tasks—one of which required him to travel to the "end of the earth." When the Greeks conceived this myth, the end of the earth was what we now know as the Strait of Gibraltar, situated between the southern tip of Spain and the northern tip of Morocco. The twin peaks on either side of the strait became known as the Pillars of Hercules, and they marked the entry into the abyss—the Atlantic Ocean.

Legend has it that the Pillars of Hercules bore the warning "Nec Plus Ultra," meaning *nothing further beyond*, as a warning to sailors not to venture into the dangerous unknown. But after Columbus discovered America, the emperor Charles V (who was also King Charles I of Spain) decided that "Plus Ultra," meaning *further beyond*, would be a more appropriate motto for his country because it would encourage others to take risks as Columbus had. *Plus Ultra*, which remains Spain's national motto to this day, is symbolized by an S-shaped scroll displaying the imperative to venture further beyond. The combination of the scroll with the twin vertical Pillars of Hercules was an inspiration for the US dollar sign: $.

Translated into modern advice for the millennial investor, the sign stands as a symbol for what you should do with your money: take the path that appears risky and uncertain, but in fact leads to great rewards. For our generation, this means investing in the global stock market early and often. Money is just like a seed. Planted, it will grow and prosper; unplanted, it will slowly die. Decisions that you make now, early in life, can mean the difference between an adequate financial outcome and an exemplary one. To see how and why, we will journey through markets, history, human behavior, demographics, globalization, and investment strategies. A combined understanding of each will allow you to build a fortune. Let's dive in.

1
——

THE MILLENNIAL EDGE

I n 2060, lifelong friends Liam and Grace are attending their fiftieth high school reunion and reminiscing about their lives. In their 68 years, they have seen the world transformed. They watched astronauts land on and colonize Mars, saw President Pierce inaugurated as the first leader of the Global Confederate States, and marveled as the robot population surpassed the human population. They also remembered tumultuous times. Both Liam and Grace had aggressive cancers in their 60s, but survived thanks to organ replacement therapy. They also lived through the student loan crisis of 2018, the Global Depression of the 2030s, the bioengineering and robotics stock bubble of 2041, and the plutonium and uranium crisis of 2050.

They both enjoyed successful careers and earned similar incomes during their working lives; Grace worked as a publisher and Liam worked in sales. Yet their lives in 2060 are very different. Grace now splits her time between New York City, Montana, and Tuscany; travels twice a year with her grandchildren; and is the chief benefactor of the Botswana Preservation Initiative. Liam lives with his son and daughter-in-law in Delaware, in a house that he helped them buy with some of his savings. He'd always wanted to retire in Oregon but, with the depletion of Social Security (the fund ran out in 2035), he had to abandon his dream and accept his son's support.

Liam and Grace's later years were so different because they took very different approaches to saving and investing. Liam, like many of his millennial contemporaries, didn't start saving in earnest until he was 40, and when he did save, he was very conservative with his money. Because he had watched his parents lose their house and go through bankruptcy, and seen his grandmother's stock portfolio decimated in the crash of 2007–2009, he was very averse to risky investments. He avoided stocks and instead built up his savings account. Because he had all his money in savings and bonds, he easily weathered the market crash of 2031, when a Global Depression hit and dragged the stock market down 75 percent. Liam thought his plan was safe and responsible, but come retirement, the purchasing power of his savings—what he could afford to buy—had eroded. He had saved more than $2,000,000, but it wasn't enough to live on comfortably. The modest apartment he hoped to buy would have cost $300,000 in 2014, but now, in 2060, cost $1,750,000.

Grace took a much different approach. She started investing once she was earning her first steady salary at age 22, taking a small amount from each paycheck and investing it in the global stock market. She continued to make investments throughout her life, even after three severe market crashes that each temporarily crippled her portfolio. After the crash of '31, she invested every spare dime she had in the market. She realized early in her career that youth trumps everything in investing, and that stocks are the only logical investment for young investors. Her choices were aggressive, and she built a sizable nest egg by the time she was 50 and a small fortune by the time she was 60.

The large ultimate divergence in lifestyle between these old friends started with two simple decisions early in their lives: when to start investing and what to buy. The choices you make today—and in the years to come—will determine whether you live like Liam or live like Grace. This chapter explains why Grace succeeded and Liam failed. Grace's secret was investing young and putting all her money into the global stock market. Liam's error was starting later and thinking that savings and conservative investments were safe when they were instead dangerous. As we shall see, fortune favors the young.

The Millennial Investor

Liam and Grace are two members of the huge millennial genera-tion. Defined as those born between 1980 and 2000, millennials make up the largest generation in history—there are 80 million of us in the United States alone. More than half of millennials have already entered the workforce, and more than 10,000 of us turn 21 every day. Unfortunately, because of the tough times that we have already lived through and the unique challenges that we will face in the future, it will be easy to fall into the same traps as Liam. Like Liam, many of us have grown up watching the stock and housing markets crash, often bringing devastation and even financial ruin to those we love. Student loans hang over our heads and good jobs are still scarce.

The tough environment in which we've grown up has had a huge impact on our investing preferences. In a 2014 survey—which compared investing preferences across generations—millennials reported a risk tolerance about as low as those in the

World War II generation.[1] We may be young and have the highest *ability* to take risks of any generation, but we are as conservative as our grandparents. In the survey, both baby boomers and Gen Xers had a higher risk tolerance than millennials. The survey report says, "Millennials are the most worried of all generations. But unlike what might be expected, their concerns are very long-term in nature—retirement and their own long-term care—issues that are decades away. They are also worried about their financial situations and avoiding making financial mistakes." Millennials responding to the survey were so conservative that, on average, they had 52 *percent* of their portfolio in cash. Even millennials with tons of money—$100,000 or more—had a 42 percent allocation to cash. Non-millennials, by contrast, had a 23 percent average allocation to cash—a much more appropriate number.[2] As the survey report says of our high cash position, "Clearly this allocation is not just based on cash needs, but reflects wariness about financial markets." This entire profile of the millennial investor should sound familiar: this is Liam's attitude writ large. In the spirit of Liam's conservative approach, millennials in the survey only had 28 percent allocated to stocks, while older generations had an average of 46 percent allocated to stocks.[3] This is a vexing contradiction, because to end up like Grace we need to own more stocks and less cash. Cash may seem safe, but as we shall see it is risky in the long run.

The good news is that young people today have more investing advantages than any group in history. Youth itself is our most important advantage, but never before have young people had such easy, cheap, and diverse access to global markets. Thanks to innovation and competition in finance, you can now buy anything you want with the click of a button. From domestic stocks, emerging market stocks, bonds, and real estate to commodities like gold, silver, palladium, wheat, corn, and livestock (and the list goes on), a huge range of investments is available to us, all for a low fee. The variety of choices can be daunting, but the simplest choices still work the best. Before explaining why stocks are the key to wealth, we must first understand why youth is such a formidable investing advantage.

Compound Returns: The Great Money Multiplier

When I was seven years old and in first grade, before realizing how destructive it could be to my playground reputation, I played competitive chess. With time to kill between tournament games, my dad would often tell me the story of the chess master and the emperor. The story went that the inventor of chess was showing the new game to his emperor and the emperor was so impressed that he offered the man any reward that he desired. The man's clever request was that the emperor place one piece of rice on the first square of the chessboard, two on the second, four on the third, and so on, doubling the rice grains until all 64 squares were filled. Trying to teach me a lesson, my dad would then give me two choices for a reward of my own: I could do the same chessboard doubling with pennies instead of rice grains, or have one million dollars. At the time, I was only able to double numbers up to 32 or 64, and much more concerned with when I was going to be able to play *Mortal Kombat* again than with his damn riddles, so I chose the million bucks. Well, when my father explained that if I'd chosen the doubling pennies I would have had $10 million by the 31st square and $92 quadrillion by the 64th, I felt pretty dumb.

This was my first lesson in the miracle of compounding, a very simple, but very powerful, bit of math. Compounding is so important for young people because each year of our lives is like a square on the chessboard—and we have a lot of spaces left ahead of us. Compounding is the engine that will make our stock portfolios grow, and time is the fuel. The key to compounding returns is that they have a much larger influence on our fortunes later in life than they do early on. Even if the *percentage* gains that we earn stay the same every year, the *dollar* gains will be much larger in later years. The doubling pennies in Table 1.1 reveal why. It takes fifteen chessboard squares to pass $100, but in the next fifteen squares the fortune grows from $163.84 to $5.4 million. Again think of each square as a year of your life. In the early squares—which represent our 20s and 30s—the dollar gains are small. But in the later squares—our 50s and 60s—the same doubling results in massive dollar gains with each new square.

Your stock investments won't ever double in value in one year, but even at much lower annual growth rates, compounding is still

Table 1.1   The Power of Compounding

Square number	Doubling pennies	Square number	Doubling pennies
1	$0.01	...16	$327.68
2	$0.02	17	$655.36
3	$0.04	18	$1,310.72
4	$0.08	19	$2,621.44
5	$0.16	20	$5,242.88
6	$0.32	21	$10,485.76
7	$0.64	22	$20,971.52
8	$1.28	23	$41,943.04
9	$2.56	24	$83,886.08
10	$5.12	25	$167,772.16
11	$10.24	26	$335,544.32
12	$20.48	27	$671,088.64
13	$40.96	28	$1,342,177.28
14	$81.92	29	$2,684,354.56
15...	$163.84	30	$5,368,709.12

a powerful force. Because the magic happens later on, the year you start investing has a huge influence on where you end up. Imagine that you and two friends all make investments in the stock market at various points in your careers and all earn the same 7 percent annual return, after inflation, that stocks have delivered across history. You start investing $10,000 per year in the stock market at age 22 and your two friends invest the same amount, but one starts at age 30 and the other at age 40. Once they start investing, each makes the same annual $10,000 investment and earns the same 7 percent annual return.[4] The only difference is time spent in the market. If you started at 22, you'd have a portfolio worth $4.7 million when you're 65. Your friend who started at age 30 would have $2.5 million, and your friend who started at 40 would have $1 million. Think of the difference in lifestyle that extra $3.7 million could buy you.

Other than time, the only other variables that could have made a difference to these hypothetical investors are the annual investment amount and the annual return. But neither higher returns nor larger investments can make up for lost time. If the 40-year-old investor somehow managed 10 percent annual returns instead of 7 percent—an enormous improvement—he'd still only finish with $1.8 million, less than half of the total you'd have earned by starting very young. If the 40-year-old investor made $20,000 annual investments instead of $10,000 investments, he'd end up with $2 million—a significant improvement from $1 million, but still well short of $4.7 million. As this example makes clear, each year is precious and there is no substitute for time. Even if you are in your 30s or 40s and haven't started investing, you should start investing now. As the Turkish proverb says, "No matter how far you have gone on the wrong road, turn back." Grace captured youth's potential, and you should too.

The Importance of Real Returns

Liam didn't fail because he was too conservative; he failed because the options that he thought were safe (his savings account and bonds) were in fact dangerous long-term investments. Savings and bonds are dangerous for millennial investors because we are the first complete generation born into a world where the value of our money has no anchor. Without an anchor, the value of each dollar (and any cash that you hold) deteriorates over time as our governments print more money. This is a relatively new problem, because from America's founding until the 1970s, dollars *did* have an anchor: each dollar was defined as some weight in gold or silver. In our lifetimes, dollars have never been fixed to anything concrete. When dollars have no anchor, inflation is a silent killer. Even in my lifetime, inflation has ruined the value of a dollar; a car that cost $10,000 when I was born in April 1985 would cost more than double that ($22,000) in 2014. Dollar devaluation is a key variable pertaining to Liam and Grace's second important decision: what to buy.

Compounding works best if you earn strong annual returns, so the next question is: where should you invest? When evaluating investment options, we have to consider returns that we can earn *after* inflation. Here's why. Let's say one month you spend $1,000 buying groceries, paying rent, and buying some new clothes. You also invest $1,000 in the stock market. Twelve months later, your portfolio has jumped to $1,100—a solid 10 percent "nominal" return. But when you go to run the same errands and pay your rent, it now costs you $1,100, $100 more than last year. In this example, inflation has destroyed your nominal return. Your "real," after-inflation return is 0 percent. While your portfolio's dollar value rose by $100, your purchasing power did not change at all. Real returns are all that matter.

Inflation is a threat for millennial investors because we live under a fiat money system; *fiat* is Latin for "let it be done." Under a fiat money system, money is "printed" or created by governments, and when more money is printed, inflation tends to rise. For most of history, money was tied to something physical and tangible like gold or silver. The modern dollar is instead an abstraction, created out of thin air. If the government continues to create billions of new dollars—thereby increasing the supply of money—then prices (inflation) will continue to drift upward over time. These price increases are a huge drag on our returns.

Millennials have always lived under a fiat system, but even so it is a fairly recent development. At various points in history, money has taken the form of paper, coins, gold, silver, salt, cattle, deerskins, vodka, ivory, wampum beads, and sperm whale's teeth. The first coins appeared in the kingdoms of Lydia and Ionia around 640 BCE. These coins were made of electrum—a naturally occurring alloy of gold and silver from a nearby river where King Midas is said to have bathed. The Incas called gold and silver "sweat of the sun" and "tears of the moon," and gold and silver have been used as money ever since. They worked so well because there is a limited supply of gold and silver in the world. Because we can't create more, each ounce of gold retains its value well. Limited quantities mean stable values and low inflation.

The history of money in the United States also began with gold and silver. At its birth in the Coinage Act of 1792, the US dollar was fixed to the price of gold and silver, meaning you could exchange one dollar for 371.25 grains of silver or 24.75 grains of gold.[5] The key advantage of a gold standard is that it acts as a check on our government's ability to create more money. More money introduced into circulation makes every dollar worth less (inflation), in that each dollar can be used to buy fewer goods and services. Figure 1.1 shows the price of an ounce of gold in US dollars since the original Coinage Act of 1792. Though the price was mostly steady for almost 200 years, there were occasions when the dollar was devalued relative to gold. The first disruption, which appears now as just a tiny blip, was the result of President Lincoln and the Union issuing $450 million dollars in paper notes known as "greenbacks" to pay for the northern army in the Civil War. The greenbacks were an early example of fiat money.

Despite brief interruptions like the Civil War and Great Depression, the gold standard lasted a long time. We even affirmed a gold standard as recently as 1944 when representatives from 44 countries met in New Hampshire to outline the post–World War II global economic landscape. In their resulting Bretton Woods Agreement, the US dollar was fixed at $35 per gold ounce. But in the early 1970s, the US economy was weak, the bill for the Vietnam War was mounting, and our government's annual spending burden had risen significantly thanks to new entitlement programs like Medicare. The government wasn't collecting enough tax money to cover all these rising expenditures, so President Nixon and his key advisers decided that the United States must end its gold standard so that it could print money at will. Nixon's decision, known as the "Nixon Shock," permanently moved the United States to a system of fiat money. In the ensuing decade, the value of the dollar plummeted against gold. At the end of 1970, an ounce of gold cost $37.60, but ten years later, in 1980, that same ounce cost $641.20—a 17-fold increase. Gold now represents but a small fraction of the money in circulation. As of July 2013, the United States holds roughly $381 billion worth of gold. That may sound like a lot, but there are more than 10 *trillion* US dollars in circulation. That means only 3.5 percent of our money is backed by gold.[6]

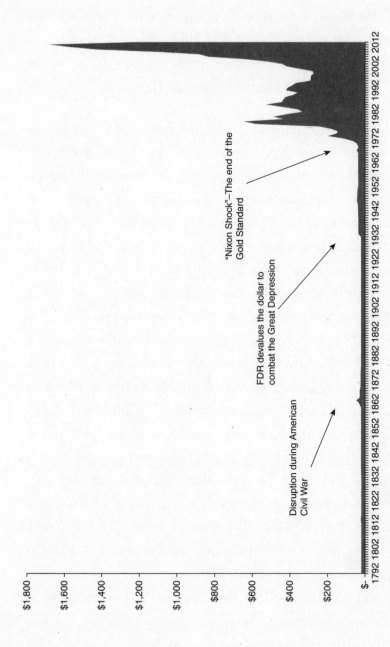

Figure 1.1   Money without Anchor. Value ($) per ounce of gold

Source: Annual gold price from Global Financial Data

The world ultimately left the gold standard because, while a gold standard does impose discipline on governments, it is inflexible. Extraordinary circumstances like major wars, depressions, and recessions demand more flexibility than a gold standard allows.

What It Means for Us

For better or worse, millennials are stuck with a fiat money system. But, as the late George Goodman (aka Adam Smith) points out, "The trouble with paper [fiat] money is that it rewards the minority that can manipulate money and makes fools of the generation that has worked and saved."[7] He could be talking about Liam's life story. What he means is that the only way to prosper under a fiat system is to park your money in investments that outpace inflation. Without such investments, your purchasing power will dwindle over time *because higher inflation slowly confiscates savings.*

The US Federal Reserve and other central banks control the amount of money in the global system and therefore have a large influence on inflation rates. Ben Bernanke, former chairman of the US Federal Reserve, has even admitted that "inflation is a tax." Inflation is here to stay, because the money supply continues to explode. Figure 1.2 shows the amount of money in circulation in the United States, in billions of dollars, between 1948 and 2013. Notice the muted growth between 1948 and 1971, when the money supply grew fourfold. Since 1971, it has exploded, growing 16-fold. There is no reason to expect this trend to slow or reverse, so inflation will remain a hidden threat to the value of our money.

Thankfully, the options that were once available only to Goodman's "minority" are now available to all. We can evaluate those options—cash, savings, bonds, and stocks—by considering their *real* returns.

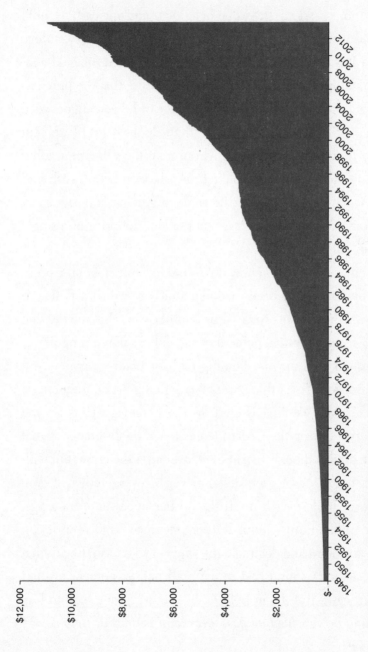

Figure 1.2   Exploding Money Supply, M2 in $billions, 1948 –2013

Source : M2 data from Global Financial Data

M2 = cash, checking deposits, savings deposits, money market mutual funds, and other time deposits.

Cash Is Trash

In a fiat money system, the value of a dollar and any cash we hold under the mattress or in our checking accounts inevitably suffers. Between 1926 and August 1971, when Nixon closed the gold window, annual inflation was 1.8 percent, meaning that the purchasing power of a dollar declined by an average of 1.8 percent per year. But since 1971, inflation has more than doubled to 4.1 percent per year. In a higher-inflation environment, the value of a dollar deteriorates faster and inflation acts as a hidden tax on cash and savings accounts. Remember, the value of a dollar is transitory. A Ford Model T cost $260 at one point, about the price of a single car tire in 2013.

Four percent inflation may not sound like much, but the problem compounds over time. A dollar that was worth a dollar in 1971 is worth 17 cents today. Put another way, this means that since 1971 more than 80 percent of the dollar's purchasing power has vanished, and anyone holding cash or holding money in a checking account over that period has suffered the consequences. That percentage decline is close to the percentage loss for the stock market during the Great Depression. The difference is that the stock market quickly began to recover after the crash, but with inflation the value of each dollar never recovers, rather, it continues to dwindle over time. Inflation has been more muted in the new millennium—about 2.4 percent since 2000—but it can strike at any point and decimate the value of your cash. Recall that in 2014, a survey found that millennials had 52 percent of their money in cash. But if you hold cash, you are guaranteed to lose purchasing power: *holding cash over long periods of time is very dangerous.*

Saving Is Not Safe

Savings accounts are better than holding cash or keeping money in a checking account. Saving sounds great, because the word connotes protection and because savings accounts pay interest. Sadly, in 2014, savings accounts are more or less worthless because the interest payments are so low. The last interest payment from my bank into my savings account was $1.63. Thanks for the coffee, Bank of America! Here I use the returns of US T-bills as a proxy for the returns earned in savings accounts. A T-bill is a very-short-term loan that someone makes to the US government, which it promises to pay back in three months, with interest. They are considered the safest investments in the world, and therefore offer low returns. Since 1926, T-bills have provided a before-inflation annual return of 3.5 percent per year. But once inflation is stripped out, that return drops to 0.5 percent, meaning that your responsibly saved dollars earn next to nothing over time.[8]

To make matters worse, over extended periods of time, there is a good chance that your savings will *lose* purchasing power, just as Liam's did. In the course of US history, T-bills have earned a negative real return in 41 percent of 50-year periods. Fifty years is a hard time frame to conceptualize, but savings are also in jeopardy over the much shorter term. Investments in T-bills have lost purchasing power in 38 percent of ten-year periods. Always remember that savings accounts will preserve the number of dollars you have, but they often fail to protect your purchasing power.

The worst-case scenario for T-bills is frightening. For the 50 years ending in April 1983, the value of one dollar shrank to 62 cents. Even the best-case scenario for real T-bill returns isn't that appealing. That dollar grew to $1.97 during the 50 years ending in December 2001.[9] That is a long time to wait for your purchasing power to double. History screams this message loud and clear: saving your money is not always safe, and simple savings accounts almost never boost your purchasing power. Even if you are a genius who switches to T-bills at the right time, you still tend to lose out in the long run. Very few investors predicted the market crash of 2008, but let's say you brilliantly foresaw that the market was going to collapse and switched to T-bills in January 2008 and held onto them until now. You'd have earned a real return of minus 8 percent through December 2013. If you'd stayed invested in stocks, you'd have earned a real gain of 27 percent through December 2013, *despite the worst market crash since the Great Depression.*

Liam built up his savings account because he thought that by doing so he would preserve his wealth and avoid the dangers of the stock market. But thanks to inflation, the true value of his savings was cut in half. To avoid Liam's fate, don't rely on simple savings.

Stocks Trump Bonds

The ultimate irony is that Grace's "risky" choice to invest in the stock market turned out to be the safest and most rewarding option. While cash and savings suffer in a world of anchorless money, stocks flourish. In real terms, stocks have outpaced all other options in every country for which we have long-term data. As seen in Table 1.2, in Norway, the United Kingdom, the United States, Germany, Japan, the Netherlands, France, Italy, Switzerland, Austria, Australia, Canada, Sweden, Denmark, Spain, Belgium, Ireland, South Africa, New Zealand, and Finland, stocks have provided positive real returns since 1900. In every one of these countries, stocks have outperformed bonds and bills—usually by wide margins.[10] And while US bills and bonds did provide positive returns after inflation during this period,

Table 1.2   After-Inflation, Real Annual Returns %

Country	1900–2012		
	Stocks	Bonds	Bills
South Africa	7.32	1.84	0.98
Australia	7.30	1.60	0.70
US	6.26	2.01	0.90
New Zealand	5.93	2.15	1.66
Canada	5.70	2.23	1.54
Sweden	5.60	2.61	1.90
UK	5.23	1.51	0.93
Finland	5.21	–0.10	–0.51
Denmark	5.01	3.18	2.16
Netherlands	4.85	1.54	0.62
Switzerland	4.25	2.21	0.81
Norway	4.13	1.85	1.16
Ireland	3.85	1.20	0.67
Japan	3.76	–1.03	–1.88
Spain	3.41	1.33	0.28
Germany	3.05	–1.71	–2.38
France	2.98	0.01	–2.81
Belgium	2.46	0.20	–0.26
Italy	1.75	–1.55	–3.64
Austria	0.63	–4.04	–8.21

bonds and bills in some other countries lost money between 1900 and 2012. Investments in supposedly "safe" short-term bills lost purchasing power in Germany, Japan, France, Italy, Belgium, Finland, and Austria. In the United States and in other countries, bills and bonds haven't helped investors build wealth.

Over long periods, stocks have always come out on top, even in the modern era of fiat money. Since the Nixon Shock, the value of the stock market has grown tenfold, while T-bills have not even doubled. That means that $100,000 invested in the stock market grew to over $1,000,000 of real purchasing power, while $100,000 in T-bills grew to just $147,000.[11]

Owning stocks means owning small slices of global companies that grow with the global economy, and that adapt to a changing economic landscape. Countless thousands of people work for the companies in the stock market, and when you become a shareholder, those people are working for you. America has been so successful because of its entrepreneurial, risk-taking spirit. People become wealthy by owning businesses. With the world working for you, your money multiplies.

To invest in the stock market, the most basic option is to buy the entire market, using cheap and easy index mutual funds or exchange-traded funds. The two most important index funds are the S&P 500, which represents 500 of America's largest companies, and the MSCI All-Country World Index, which represents thousands of global companies. The modern investor thinks of owning the entire market as natural and easy, yet some index funds are younger than many millennials. Index funds are a good starting point for owning stocks because they have very low fees and are almost always available in retirement plans. In later chapters, we will see that there are better options than index funds, but owning a piece of the overall market is still a good starting point for understanding your young money's potential.

Recall that the best-case scenario for T-bills was a doubling of your purchasing power over a 50-year span. For stocks, the *worst-case* scenario for every dollar invested in the overall market (as reflected by the S&P 500), was an eightfold return, with one dollar turning into $8.45 in real terms over 50 years. During the *average* 50-year stretch, one dollar grew to $30.31, and in the best-case scenario a dollar grew to $96.91. The power of compounding in the stock market may not be as powerful as doubling pennies on the chessboard, but it is the closest thing we have to a real-world money multiplier.

Stocks are thought of as risky because they bounce up and down a lot more than other investment options. As a stock market investor, Grace had to stick her neck out and endure some very tough times. But over a long-term holding period, the broad stock market is the *safest* place for your money. The United States stock market has provided positive real returns in every single 20-year period for which we have data. Even if you piled all your money into the market the month before the great crash of 1929, you still would have made money 20 years later. In 2013, some people are wary of the market because it has done *too* well—it is up 130 percent from the market bottom in March 2009. Some are even saying that the market is in a bubble similar to 1929, 2000, and 2007. In the face of these concerns, remember that there will never be a perfect time to buy, but even if you buy at the worst times, stocks still deliver positive real returns over time.

Buy Stocks. Start Now

We may never land on Mars or cure every cancer. There may not be another Great Depression, or another energy crisis, or a bioengineering bubble. But no matter what the future holds, you will succeed if you start investing in the market at a young age. Most people don't bother with investing until their 40s, but if we wait until later in our careers, we will squander the power of compounding returns and miss out on the potential for huge accumulation of wealth later in life. Liam thought he had saved responsibly, but was undone by a hidden force that demolished his savings. Grace recognized youth's potency and ultimately prospered. Like Grace's road to riches, ours will also be bumpy, so we will explore some of these potential obstacles in the next chapter. But by any measure, Grace's is the more desirable path. By making the right choices now, you can follow in her footsteps.

2

BUILDING GOOD FINANCIAL KARMA

I learned one very important lesson in high school: karma can be a bitch. I went to a school with more than 3,500 students and it was very easy to get lost in the crowd. Rather than working hard and investing in my future, I did the bare minimum. I figured a B (or, let's be honest, a B-) average and a good SAT score would be sufficient to get accepted to some decent colleges. To camouflage my laziness, I'd control how and when my parents saw my grades. For several years my parents didn't even know that my high school sent out interim report cards. I would steal them from the mailbox, dispose of them, and then in a panic work my Cs and Ds up to Bs in time for the real report card. This ruse was up when my high-achieving sister joined me in high school and insisted that my parents see her straight-A report cards at midterm—exposing my mediocrity in the process.

One morning in spring 2003, when seniors were starting to hear back from colleges, my father called me as I was waking up at a friend's house. He told me to come home because several slim envelopes had come for me in the mail. I dragged myself home, head pounding, and learned that I'd been rejected by every school to which I had applied. No waiting lists, no more letters still to come; 100 percent rejection, all at once. I realize that in the scheme of things, this isn't that great a hardship, but it was my first very valuable lesson in cause and effect. I learned that what you do in the present reverberates into the future. My measly investment in my high school education had come back to haunt me in the form of five small envelopes.

The word karma has simple origins. In Sanskrit, it means action or a deed done. Karma isn't some mystical, abstract concept—it's just cause and effect. My early experience with rejection taught me that karma is one of the most important facts of life—every action (or inaction) has a consequence; as ye sow, so shall ye reap. I was determined from that point forward to never again choose laziness and avoidance, but instead to act in the present in ways that would echo positively into the future. This chapter is about two kinds of financial karma: individual and collective. Building good individual financial karma is straightforward: spend less than you earn and invest a chunk of your income in the stock market every year. It is more complicated for an entire country like the United States to build good karma because it is hard for a collective group, with different and often competing individual interests, to think long term. Lucky for us, building good individual karma will overcome the consequences of bad collective karma.

Paying Yourself Is Good Karma

Early investments are little bits of positive financial karma. To make this easier to understand, let's think about playing the lottery. If you are like me, you have an occasional lottery fantasy. Often I'll be driving somewhere and I'll be reminded by a Powerball billboard that with a little bit of luck I could win $100 million. After seeing a billboard, my brain takes me on a whirlwind tour of post-jackpot splendor, where a boat ushers my wife and me to some exotic location, or a fancy car sits parked in my mansion's garage—you know the drill—before traffic jolts me back to reality. Buying lottery tickets is a bad idea, but some people do get lucky. Imagine the story of a long-suffering lottery player, Mr. Moneypenny. Six Powerball tickets cost $12. Your odds of winning are minuscule (about 1 in 175 million for each ticket), but the game remains popular. Mr. Moneypenny has been playing the lottery his entire life: buying six tickets a day, every day, from age 25 until right before retirement, when thanks to a bit of outrageous fortune he wins the lottery and bags $1 million. Any lifelong lottery player would be thrilled with this outcome. But you can achieve the same outcome as Mr. Moneypenny without any luck whatsoever. If Mr. Moneypenny had invested the same amount—$12 per day, $4,380 per year—starting at age 25, and the overall market had a return similar to its long-term historical return (7 percent after inflation), then he would have had the same $1,000,000 at age 65.

Four thousand per year is a lot of money to save at age 25, especially when jobs are scarce and student-loan debts loom—but to build long-term wealth you must make short-term sacrifices. If you're willing to undertake even more personal austerity (with the potential to grow very wealthy), it can be as simple as contributing the maximum to your 401(k) or similar retirement plan every year. In 2013, the maximum contribution for 401(k) plans is $17,500—a huge chunk of the median salary for a 25 year old. But consider this: if you maximize your 401(k) contributions from age 25 through retirement and earn a normal market return along the way, you'll have $6.6 million dollars by age 65.[1] More important are your *early* contributions. Time is a key element for financial karma because of the already explored miracle of compounding. The same $17,500 invested annually starting at age 40—when most people are more likely to be thinking about investing for retirement—would grow to $1.8 million by age 65, a fraction of the $6.6 million. Deciding how much to invest is a personal decision, but I believe in paying yourself a tithe—10 percent of your income—or, if you can manage it, as much as 20 percent. I also recommend setting up automatic contributions to your retirement accounts, since this increases the chance that you will stick to your investment plan.

Following this plan will set you up for individual financial success, but it will also protect you from future problems that may arise as the result of bad collective karma. Predicting what problems may lay ahead is difficult, but there are some key trends which we can forecast. We turn now to trends in income inequality, demographics, government support programs, and debt—all of which will play a large role in our generation's future. Understanding the potential challenges ahead will encourage young people to start investing now so that when these obstacles appear, they are small bumps on the road to financial prosperity.

Overcoming Income Inequality

One of my earliest concrete memories was watching Bill Clinton campaign for president in the early 1990s. The '90s were a prosperous decade, but from the time that President Clinton took office in 1993 through the end of 2011, the average American only got a 13 percent raise. Not 13 percent per year—13 percent *total*, after adjusting for inflation. Imagine if your salary grew 13 percent between 2014 and 2032; that is not the future any of us envision for ourselves. A 13 percent raise over such a long period stinks, but the story gets worse if you remove the income increases earned by the top 1 percent, who earned a whopping 57.5 percent raise over the same period. If you remove the top earners, income for the bottom 99 percent grew by just 5.8 percent after inflation. This recent stagnation is a continuation of a longer-term trend. Between 1974 and 2011, real income rose by a tiny 3.2 percent for the vast majority of Americans, while real income grew by 154 percent for the top earning 1 percent.[2] If this trend continues, it could be a big problem for our nascent generation of workers.

Luckily, there is a simple solution. An investment in the stock market in 1974—the beginning of this period of income stagnation—would have made the growth of income for even the top earners look pedestrian. Between 1974 and 2011, when the average worker barely earned a raise, the stock market grew by a real *759 percent*. If you narrow the window to the post-Clinton period between 1993 and 2011, the stock market grew by a real 162 percent, trumping the 57.5 percent income growth rate for the top 1 percent. This post-1993 stock market growth happened despite *two* of the worst market crashes that we have ever seen, in 2000 and 2008, when the stock market twice declined more than 40 percent. As this example makes clear, the stock market is upward mobility writ large. Even if income inequality persists as a problem for American society, we can overcome low income growth with strong portfolio growth.

Demographics Are Destiny

Using demographic data—which measure the characteristics of entire populations and specific generations—is a great way to forecast our economic and political future. Demographics tell us how many people are born each year and therefore how many people there will be in various age groups in the future. The current data tells us that as our population gets older, governments and working people (especially millennials) will bear a great burden to support elderly populations. For millennials, this could mean higher taxes, lower government benefits, and a postponed retirement.

We go through several important stages in our lives, from young dependents, to young ambitious earners, to the apex of our careers and earnings, and then again into a state of dependence in our old age. The healthiest distribution of a population is one which is skewed younger, with more young and apex earners to support those who cannot fully support themselves. Support of retired Americans has become one of the primary functions of the US government, and many retirees are dependent on government benefits. Because we millennials are such a large generation, our future tax dollars will be one of the primary means of funding government programs designed to support those in need, elderly and otherwise.

One key to continued prosperity for any country is the fertility rate, or the average number of children per woman. To maintain a population, a nation must average 2.1 children per woman. If a country's fertility rate is below 2.1, then that country's population will decline and get older, which means fewer productive workers and an elderly population which is more expensive to support. Unfortunately, most developed countries around the world have fertility rates well below the ideal rate of 2.1. Japan and Italy, with rates of 1.4, are in particularly bad shape.[3] With rates this low, the populations of Japan and Italy may decline by 50 percent or more within the next 45 years. It has already gotten so bad in Japan that in 2011 more adult diapers were sold than baby diapers.[4]

At 1.9, the American fertility rate is far healthier than most of the developed world.[5] Despite our advantage relative to other major countries, we are still far from the fertility highs last seen in 1960 when, at the tail end of the baby boom, our fertility rate was 3.7. *The consequence of a declining fertility rate is an aging population, and an aging population requires much more spending to support.* Because the aging baby boom is such a massive generation, the United States is growing much older. From 2013 to 2025, the number of Americans aged 65 and older will have grown by 72 percent.[6] This growth represents a remarkable transformation of human demographics and life expectancy. Sixty-five years or older used to be an abnormally long life, but now this cohort is the fastest-growing population segment. Our Cro-Magnon ancestors enjoyed just 18 years of life on average, and by 1726 life expectancy had risen to just 25.3 years.[7] An American born in 1900 had a life expectancy of just 47, and a meager 4.1 percent of people lived past their 65th birthday, so retirement wasn't a pressing concern.[8] But by 2013, life expectancy had jumped to 79, and the majority of people were living past their 65th birthday and enjoying a long (and expensive) retirement. The explosion of life expectancy is one of the great modern achievements—and I for one hope the trend continues—but it is a double-edged sword. As baby boomers continue to retire over the next 20 years, the population of retirees will outnumber the number of young people under the age of 20. This demographic change will result in a median age in our country that is similar to what Florida's is today.[9] The joke that Florida is death's waiting room won't be as funny anymore. Supporting this growing group of retirees will be a burden on us.

An Intergenerational Heist

There are many ways that our government supports those older than 65, but I am going to focus on the two broadest and largest: Social Security and Medicare. These programs began during the administrations of President Franklin Roosevelt (Social Security) and President Lyndon Johnson (Medicare) to support the welfare of the American population by providing steady income and health care. The cost of these programs is tied to the aging of the American population. More old people living long lives means a great burden for the government.

Millennials now represent 25 percent of the American population, and we will play a crucial role in funding these programs (should they continue to exist) during our peak earning years.[10] To see why, we can project how many working Americans between the ages of 20 and 64 there will be at various points in the future to support each retired person over 65. The lower this ratio, the larger the burden on each active worker. Figure 2.1 reveals the heavy burden that millennials will bear. In 1950, there were 7 working-age people supporting every person 65 and older. The ratio declined to 5 workers per retiree in 2000, but it is about to take a nosedive. Baby boomers began to reach retirement in 2010, when we had 4.5 workers per retiree, but as they continue to retire and live long lives, the number will fall all the way to 2.7 by 2030 and continue to decline below two workers per retiree thereafter.[11]

Money to pay for government support programs comes in large part from working taxpayers, and the greatest burden, in terms of the tax dollars that we will be paying, will fall on millennials during our peak earning years between 2030 and 2050.[12] This is important for two reasons. First, if these programs continue in their current form our tax rates will have to go up because there will be fewer Americans working to support each retiree. Second, there is a serious risk that these aid programs will buckle under the pressure of their rising costs, and we will no longer be able to afford them. In the latter scenario, it is possible that we will continue to pay our dues into the system, but receive reduced benefits

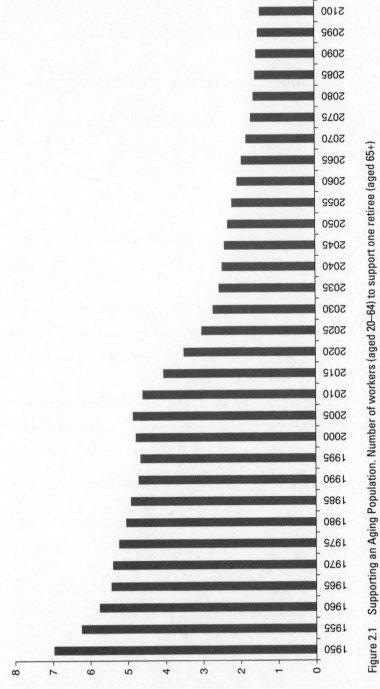

Figure 2.1 Supporting an Aging Population. Number of workers (aged 20–64) to support one retiree (aged 65+)

Source: http://esa.un.org/unpd/wpp/Excel-Data/population.htm, data from table "Old-Age Dependency Ratio 2"; author's calculations for number of workers to cover those aged 65+

from the system later in life. Both concerns are reasons for us to invest (not just save) more now, so that we will have a large portfolio to offset higher taxes and/or lower government benefits.

Spending, Savings, and Debt

The American government has changed considerably since its inception. The promise it first made to Americans was life, liberty, and the pursuit of happiness. Now, the government makes many more promises to its citizens, including income and health care in retirement. These have had a profound impact on our relationship with our government and may help explain why the personal savings rate (a proxy for individual karma) has steadily declined over the years, so much so that more than half of retirees end their careers with less than $50,000 saved.[13] In the first year following World War II, our government spent the equivalent of 2.5 percent of our country's total economic output (gross domestic product, GDP) on "human resources," a spending category now dominated by Social Security and Medicare. In 2012, spending on human resources was 15.1 percent of the nation's GDP. To put this change in perspective, spending on national defense was 5.5 percent of GDP in 1947—the first year that spending fell off after the spike created by World War II—and hasn't changed much since: it was 4.4 percent of GDP in 2012.[14] Figure 2.2 shows that while Social Security and Medicare have become a larger and larger percentage of federal spending, the savings rate has been cut in half.

The primary concern for our generation is the sustainability of programs like Social Security and Medicare. For Americans of all ages, it is comforting to think that our basic needs like income and health care will be funded by the government, but such thinking also discourages savings and investment. A low savings rate means

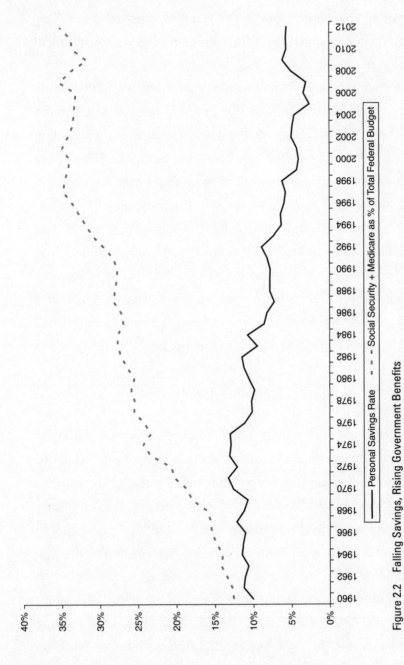

Figure 2.2 Falling Savings, Rising Government Benefits

Source: Medicare and Social Security spending from http://www.whitehouse.gov/omb/budget/historicals, Table 3.1; personal savings rate from the Bureau of Economic Analysis

that US citizens will have to be *more* reliant on the government in the future, not less. If we want to enjoy government support when our turn comes, then we must know whether or not these programs are sustainable for the future and how the government plans to fund them.

We've already seen that wealth inequality has gotten worse in the United States, so often the cry is to increase taxes on the wealthiest. Higher taxes on the rich may help matters, but in our case, the redistribution has also been money borrowed from creditors—China and others—and given to American citizens. In 2012 alone, the United States borrowed more than $1 trillion to fund government spending—the fourth straight year above $1 trillion. The United States has accumulated $17 trillion in debt, and almost a third of that accumulation ($5.4 trillion) occurred between 2008 and 2012. Debt is bad karma, because what you borrow now must be paid back later. America borrowed a ton and accumulated significant bad collective karma in the process.

Looming Debt

America already owes $17 trillion to its creditors, yet in addition to this official debt there is also a dangerous gap between what our government has promised to pay in benefits in the future (through Social Security and Medicare) and what it expects to earn in taxes in the future. This gap is known as the fiscal gap. Any spending costs not covered by incoming tax receipts must be funded through debt. Most of the rising costs are due to our aging population, so if the promises made by our government to the aging baby boomers are kept, we cannot escape these rising costs. One extreme estimate is that the fiscal gap is $222 *trillion* dollars or $710,000 for every man, woman, and child in America.[15] The system would crumble well before the country reached such an outrageous debt level, but the $222 trillion estimate highlights why growing government spending is dangerous.

The bill is so massive because funding the baby boomers' retirement is going to be expensive. They will likely receive more in benefits than they paid into the system in taxes, to a degree that we might dub them the "dine-and-dash" generation. This will not sit well with millennials as we ourselves get older and continue to pay taxes. The proverbial "kicking the can down the road" can't last forever, and already organizations like The Can Kicks Back are being founded by millennials to fight back on this issue. Either taxes or spending will have to change, or our national debt will grow to be greater than our GDP. Ideally, we'd implement a plan that allowed us to pay down our debt rather than expand it, but this is very hard to do. Even if we wanted to *maintain* our current debt level, relative to our country's GDP, the Congressional Budget Office estimates that total tax revenues would have to rise by 25 percent or government spending would have to fall by 20 percent.[16] But government spending doesn't often fall, and certainly not by 20 percent. It's risen at an 8 percent annual rate since 1940, and it's fallen in just 9 of the last 73 years, 3 of which were the years winding down from the high spending years during World War II. That means higher taxes are much more likely.

There is such a thing as responsible debt. A mortgage makes home ownership possible, and is usually a responsible use of debt because the borrower pays off the loan over time with income earned. Across US history, our debt load—what our government owes to creditors—has spiked around wartime because it is so expensive to fund a war. These occasions, too, were responsible uses of debt because our safety as a nation was on the line. Just as a mortgage is supported by the borrower's income, so too should our national debt be supported by our economic output and the taxes it generates. But the United States has grown addicted to borrowing, and given how unlikely it is that it can repay its debts, its borrowing has become irresponsible.

A False Sense of Security

For Ida May Fuller, who retired in 1939 and lived to age 100, the Social Security program worked out quite nicely. She paid a total of $24.75 into the system, but received $22,888 in benefits over her very long life. The idea behind the program is to provide a safety net in retirement, funded by contributions from each worker over his or her career. The funding comes through FICA (Federal Insurance Contributions Act), or payroll taxes, paid by both employees and employers in every pay cycle. As the number of retirees has increased over the years, the government has raised the FICA tax rate to cover the higher benefits that it has paid out. The rate was just 2 percent in the 1930s (1 percent each from employee and employer), and has risen to today's current rate of 15.3 percent, prompting basketball star Shaquille O'Neal to ask "Who the hell is FICA? When I meet him, I am going to punch him in the face."

This system should work so long as money taken in through taxes meets or exceeds money paid out in benefits. For most of its history, the Social Security Administration has paid out less than it has taken in and has used these surpluses to build up a so-called trust fund, which can be used to cover the program in future years when it is paying out more than it charges in taxes. The problem is that this trust fund is just not a fund at all but an accounting gimmick. There is no dedicated account sitting somewhere in Washington with the accumulated money. Future obligations to retirees are from the US government, not from a trust fund, and the government is deep in debt. According to the Social Security board of trustees themselves, in 2013, there is a $9.6 trillion dollar gap between what Social Security will have to pay out in the next 75 years and what it expects to take in through taxes, measured in today's dollars. Their estimate just one year earlier was $8.6 trillion. If you extend the horizon beyond those 75 years and assume the program goes on forever to support our children and grandchildren, then the unfunded liability becomes $23.1 trillion. There are only a few ways to fund an unfunded liability—more taxes or more borrowing. Neither is good for us.

Attack of the Struldbrugs

In his famous travels, Gulliver meets a group of immortals known as Struldbrugs. Theirs is a rather depressing variety of immortality because, while they do live forever, they continue to age and decay. Struldbrugs are a nuisance to the mortal population; after a while, old Struldbrugs cannot even communicate because the language changes over time and Struldbrugs do not adapt. After meeting the Struldbrugs, immortality's original appeal wanes for Gulliver, and he learns that we should be careful what we wish for. We all want to live as long as possible, but longer lives are much more expensive.

The US population is aging and its support system (active workers per retiree) will continue to decline, so we must be concerned that the current system—and therefore current benefits—will not be viable when we retire. Health care is especially important for an aging population with fewer workers to support health care costs. The details of our health care policy and system are too complicated to explore in detail, but the important point for young investors is that, like Social Security, the costs of this program may grow so prohibitive that our government cannot offer the same support to us when we are elderly and in need of care.

Medicare costs have no ceiling, and health care costs have grown at an astonishing pace. Since it began in 1966, Medicare spending has grown by 11 percent per year—a far greater rate than the 6.4 percent growth rate for non-Medicare federal spending.[17] While the rate has slowed somewhat in the past 15 years, the retiring baby boom generation will spike costs over the coming decades as the 65-and-over population jumps by 40 million people.[18]

For Medicare, the unfunded liability in 2013 was $4.6 trillion, but that is assuming that assets in the so-called Medicare trust fund are used to pay off much of the future liabilities.[19] Again, there is no separate account full of cash waiting to cover this shortfall. Starting in 2008 and in each year since, Medicare spending has exceeded income—and as the baby boom retirement kicks into high gear, the need to spend even more will be suffocating.[20] As the global population gets older, we face our own Struldbrug problem. Comparing our elderly to Struldbrugs is a bit insensitive, but there is no escaping the costs associated with age and longer lives, and those costs may decrease the support that millennials receive in the future.

Things That Can't Go On, Stop

Each year, the Congressional Budget Office issues a report on our country's long-term fiscal health. The report details two scenarios—a base line and an alternative scenario. Following the alternative scenario—which many analysts believe to be more appropriate—Medicare and Social Security are unsustainable because the government would have to borrow too much money to fund them.[21] *According to the CBO analysis, if the United States continues on its current path, it would owe more than twice its GDP by 2037.* Rises in costs come from either higher cost per person per year, or more years lived. For both Social Security and Medicare, the aging population is the main driver of the increase in future costs. Cost per person per year is also expected to rise—mostly for Medicare—so the main driver is not aging alone. Congress could cut spending per retiree, but it cannot pass a bill that reduces the number of old people.[22] As costs rise, remember that government—and what it offers us as citizens—can change dramatically over short periods. Both of my living grandparents were born before our major support programs came into existence. My parents, who are both 53, were born before Medicare. The United States government's transformation has happened very fast. If necessary, it could be undone just as fast, leaving our generation much less secure in our later years.

The unraveling may have already begun, because as spending has risen the quality of governance in America has deteriorated. Since 1996, the World Bank has tracked the quality of governments around the world using five key measures: control of corruption, government effectiveness, political stability, regulatory quality, and the extent to which the government is accountable to its citizens. Between 1996 and 2011, the United States deteriorated in *each* of the five categories. Even worse, of the 45 key countries in the global stock market, only seven have had a larger deterioration in the quality of their governments.[23] And of those same 45 countries, only six other countries deteriorated in all five categories, including Greece, Italy, and Egypt.[24] We are in some bad company.

Bad governance and a mountain of debt is a scary combination. In my favorite '90s comedy, *Dumb and Dumber,* Lloyd and his partner Harry come across a briefcase filled with cash and spend it all. When the crook who lost the briefcase confronts Lloyd, Lloyd says "My friend Harry and I have every intention of fully reimbursing you." They hand back the crook's briefcase, which is now full of scraps of paper. "What is this?! Where's all the money?!" asks the crook. "That's as good as money sir, those are IOUs," answers Lloyd, "Go ahead and add it up, every cent accounted for. Look, you see this? 275 thou'... might wanna hang on to that one!" The United States is accumulating IOUs just like Lloyd and Harry. It can't keep handing IOUs from one generation to the next. At some point—which we may have already reached—the debts will be too large, the music will stop, and younger generations will suffer. As a group, the country hasn't thought long term. It's borrowed from future generations, even unborn generations, to pay for cushy benefits for current beneficiaries. Karma is cause and effect. If America continues to borrow like mad now, it will suffer later. We must counteract bad karma with good by improving our individual positions.

The Easy Fix

The worst-case scenario would be that we pay our FICA taxes throughout our careers and then receive zero or reduced benefits when we retire. Without preparation through investing, this would be a disaster as we'd be left with no means to support ourselves and no way to pay for medical care. But early investments in the stock market can overcome this dire scenario. Let's imagine Ida May Fuller was retiring today at age 65 and lives to 85, which is the current average life expectancy for a woman who reaches 65. Over those twenty years, if she collected the maximum monthly Social Security benefits, she'd receive $30,396 per year and total lifetime benefits of $607,920. To have $607,920 at age 65, you'd only have to invest around $3,000 per year, starting at age 25. I wish I could present these numbers to every single American, in person. I think that if I did, the savings rate would bounce back to longer-term norms, and everyone would begin to better invest for their future.

While this chapter has explored important demographic and political trends, the rest of the book leaves these topics behind because they are beyond our direct control. Investing for our own future, on the other hand, is something we control. Smart and responsible investing is similar to smart and responsible health: it involves accepting a deferred benefit. Eat a healthy diet now and enjoy good health in the future. Invest now and reap the rewards later in life. Thomas Edison said that "The doctor of the future will give no medicine, but instead will interest his patients in the care of human frame, in diet, and in the cause and prevention of disease." Sadly, long after Edison's prediction, we have still not embraced preventive care, neither for our physical nor for our financial health. We need to do things differently. Preventive care in investing is simple. We just have to commit to it now.

Rolling with the Punches

Things will continue to change, but the beautiful thing about the stock market is that it adapts. Companies rise to capitalize on new trends, new technologies, or new economic environments. Because the stock market involves constant feedback, it changes with the times. When my great-grandfather was 11 years old in 1896, the twelve most important companies in the United States were American Cotton Oil, American Sugar, American Tobacco, Chicago Gas, Distilling & Cattle Feeding, General Electric, Laclede Gas, National Lead, North American, Tennessee Coal Iron and RR, U.S. Leather, and United States Rubber. These were the original members of the Dow Jones Industrial Average (DJIA), a list of stocks created by the *Wall Street Journal* and Charles Dow to help track the stock market's performance. The DJIA has added and subtracted companies over the years as industries and companies have thrived or petered out. General Electric alone has stood the test of time, a remarkable accomplishment. Where American Sugar and United States Rubber once reigned in the stock market, Google and Apple now dominate. They too may fall, but if you are invested in the stock market, you will benefit from the stocks that replace them. As we've seen, it pays to be invested in such an adaptive system.

Any success story includes hardship. Our generation will face several obstacles as we continue to advance in our careers. We may pay a large sum in taxes to support key government aid programs, but then not receive similar benefits to those enjoyed by previous generations. There will be fewer active workers to support more retirees, and we will be the ones to bear that heavy load. But even in the face of hardship, we will still author our successes and our failures. We can summarize the topics discussed in this chapter by considering a few real (after-inflation) growth rates. Since 1967, the second year of Medicare spending, real income has grown by just 0.5 percent per year, government spending has grown by 2.9 percent, and benefit spending on Social Security and Medicare has grown by 4.7 percent—and baby boomers are just beginning to retire. During the same period, the savings rate has fallen from 12.2 percent to 5.6 percent. But the stock market, our upward mobility machine, has trumped all of these rates, growing by 5.1 percent per year, after inflation. The market has had its hardships too, declining by 40 percent or more on three separate occasions, yet it continues to trot upward, riding industry, free markets, and human ingenuity to new highs. The same wave will carry us into our future.

The remedy to our problems is simple. First, start investing now by setting up an automatic contribution to your retirement account, your investment account, or both. Start with 10 percent and go higher when you can. Second, control your spending. The 10 percent goal will require some personal austerity. Just remember that spending tends to expand with your income level unless you protest and take action to control yourself. Finally, with your growing investment account, make long-term investments in the global stock market. This plan will build enough good personal karma to counteract any bad collective karma that we've accumulated. Financial karma wills out, so start building yours now.

3

—

INVESTING PRINCIPLES

N ow that we've covered why it is so important to make regular contributions to your investment account, we can focus on the fun part: how to invest. The remainder of this book is devoted to three investing principles. By following these three principles, you can build a portfolio that harnesses the power of the stock market to grow your wealth, while at the same time protecting you from any future inflation, dollar devaluation, or overreliance on government support programs.

Three Ingredients

I'm a novice cook, but my sister is a trained and very creative chef. Whenever we're in the kitchen together, I like to watch and learn. Some of her best recipes were wasted on me, though—they had too many ingredients so I could not replicate her results. When I made this complaint to her several times, she started creating recipes that I could manage. She kept the ingredients simple and the techniques basic. The new recipes are just as delicious, but now I get to enjoy great food more often because I can do it myself. Investing is just like cooking: the best recipes are the simplest ones, with few ingredients and simple techniques. If things get too complicated, we tend to get lost. Because simple is better, my investing recipe has three ingredients: *go global, be different,* and *get out of your own way.* That is all you need to know to achieve impressive returns. The rest of this book explores these three elements in detail, but first here's a summary of what each means for your portfolio.

Go Global. Investors tend to concentrate their portfolios in stocks based in their home country, but you should instead build a global portfolio by buying stocks in different regions and countries around the world. US investors, for example, have a vast majority of their portfolios invested in American stocks. This is a big mistake because it concentrates risk in one place and ignores many great opportunities abroad. The tendency to overweight one's home country is common to investors around the world. British investors prefer stocks from the United Kingdom and Canadian investors overweight Canadian stocks in their portfolios. We Americans prefer domestic companies because we are more familiar with them, use their products, and can see their CEOs on the national news. Yet the companies we usually think of as local (be they American or otherwise) are in fact global. General Electric—one of the oldest stocks in the world—earns more than half of its revenue outside the United States. This is also true of many other large, well-known American companies. As an individual investor, you need to follow GE's lead by investing your money outside your own borders. Going global means we can select from a larger set of stocks, protect ourselves from a potentially weak US dollar (or other local currency), and take advantage of emerging market economies.

Be Different. To achieve investing greatness by performing even better than the market, you must build a portfolio that is different from the overall stock market. The dominant trend in investing today is toward "index" or "passive" strategies, which allow investors to own every major stock in a given market for a very low fee. Passive index investing has become so popular because it is difficult to beat a simple index; more and more investors are buying index funds. As a result, everyone's portfolios are starting to look a lot alike and perform about the same. While the index approach certainly has its merits, there is a better way.

With the right strategy and the right discipline, you can beat the overall market. The strategy that I outline in chapters 5 and 6 will give millennial investors a true edge. It was not until very recently that investors had the means to take advantage of this strategy on a global scale, and ours is the first generation that can capitalize on this edge from an early age. Think about genetics for a moment. Some people are more prone to athletic excellence, others to heart disease. Stocks, just like people, have genes. Some stocks are more likely to outperform the market; others are more likely to underperform it. The best way to be different is to only own stocks with the best genes—the ones that are the most likely to outperform in the future. Good genes are things like cheap prices and strong earnings; bad genes are things like expensive prices and reckless corporate spending.

Index strategies only care about one gene: size. They own companies according to how big they are, so any index investor owns a ton of Apple and ExxonMobil stock, but owns much less stock of competitors Hewlett-Packard and Hess Corporation. This strategy is flawed because bigger does not mean better in the stock market. You should instead own companies because they are cheap, because they are smart with their cash, and because, while they have been neglected, the market is just starting to notice them. The overall global stock market is a great place to put your money and is the key to wealth—but owning stocks with the special characteristics that I will discuss will grow your money at a faster clip than a simple index fund.

Get Out of Your Own Way. The most important—and perhaps most difficult—element of this plan is mastering your emotions so that you don't make common mistakes that would sidetrack you and your portfolios. Human software (our culture) has grown at a far greater pace than human hardware (our biology). Our brains and our bodies are not much different from those of the *Homo sapiens* that dwelled in the caves of Pinnacle Point in South Africa 164,000 years ago—but our world is drastically different. Cultural and technological evolution are extremely fast, so cultural constructs like the stock market confound our brains; everything that worked for survival in the savannah leads to extinction in the markets.

Take running from danger. It's a great strategy if you're being chased by a pack of lions, but running (by selling out of the market) is a terrible strategy if you find yourself panicking in the middle of a market crash. Because we are biologically programmed to fail as investors, it is essential that young investors learn the right way of doing things before the market overwhelms us. It will be much easier to choose the right path early in your career, when you don't have much invested, and when you haven't faced the emotional market gauntlet. This will be easier said than done—it is much easier to be brave from a safe distance. Still, with the right preparation, you can conquer your emotions and beat the market. I will explore how and why we are programmed to make investing mistakes, and why you should set up automatic contributions to your investment account, ignore feelings of greed and fear, and force yourself to focus on the long term.

If you follow this simple recipe, you will succeed. Now we can explore each element in detail. First up: why, in the modern world, you must build a global portfolio.

4

——

GO GLOBAL

I was born in Minneapolis, Minnesota, in 1985, and I will be 29 years old when this book is published. While the timing and location of my birth were beyond my control, they have shaped my life story. In this book I've written a lot about the US stock market because I am an American and because our market has performed so well for so long. But what if, instead, I had been born in Tokyo in 1960 and wrote a book at the same age in 1989 arguing that young people should invest in the stock market? In this alternate universe, I would have focused on the Japanese stock market, since the Nikkei (the major Japanese index) was dominating the world at that time. The Nikkei was up 30 percent in 1989, capping a decade where it rose by a whopping 500 percent. In the late 1980s, Japanese corporate dominance was convincing even mighty Americans that their top economic position was in jeopardy. I went through a Michael Crichton phase when I was younger and I loved his novel *Rising Sun*, a murder mystery set amidst a Japanese take-over of corporate America. The novel's plot is hard to imagine in hindsight, but in the late 1980s it seemed that the Land of the

Rising Sun was poised to dominate the global economy. Japanese investors were buying up American companies and real estate at breakneck speed. The Mitsui Corporation spent a record $610 million to purchase the Exxon Building in New York City, reportedly paying $260 million above Exxon's asking price just so that it could set a world record.[1] Other major American landmarks and brands, like Rockefeller Center and Colombia Records, were also acquired by large Japanese firms.

My book would have detailed how investments in the Nikkei could allow investors to get rich and enjoy the spoils of a long, sustained bull market. My argument would have been convincing because Japan had all the trappings of a booming economy and bullish stock market. Japanese real estate was worth four times the entire real estate value of the United States. The value of French Impressionist paintings shot up 20-fold in just 15 years thanks to their popularity among wealthy Japanese buyers. It cost 400 million yen ($2.7 million) to join the top golf club in Tokyo, and more than $1 million to join many others.[2] My book might have been a bestseller, because times were good and everyone was getting rich in the Japanese stock market.

But the book would have turned out to be a disaster, because in 1990 the Nikkei tanked—and (as I write in 2013) has yet to recover. The fundamental problem was that in 1989 the Japanese market was outrageously overpriced. At its peak, the market was trading at 90 times profits (corporate earnings), a valuation seldom seen across global market history. Certain Japanese industries traded at even more ridiculous prices—fishery and forestry companies traded at 319 times earnings. To put this in perspective, if an enterprising youngster in your family ran a lemonade stand that earned $50 a day, 365 days a year, his or her lemonade "business" would be worth $5.8 million dollars with a similar valuation.

The market was off its rocker. In comparison, America's S&P 500 traded at 30 times profits in March 2000, at the absolute peak of the technology bubble that was among the most speculative and irrational market bubbles in history. From its overblown market peak in 1990 through 2013, the Japanese market is down 44 percent.[3] A Japanese investor who invested in the Nikkei in 1989—and who believed that equities were the surest path to wealth—would have half of her money left 24 years later.

This cautionary tale is an important one, because while stock markets tend to do very well over time, individual markets can perform very poorly for long periods. To control for this risk, you should never place too big a bet on stocks in your home country. I am writing as an American investor and, while the US market is nowhere near as expensive in early 2014 as the Japanese market was in 1989, there is no way to know what lies ahead for my domestic market. The combination of our country's fiat currency system, the limitless debt this system has allowed the country to accumulate, and its aging population may mean that the returns we earn in the future may not match those we have seen in the past. Back to the hypothetical Japanese version of my book. Following the Nikkei's strong performance in the 1980s, I would have been inclined to tell investors to put their money in the domestic Japanese market—terrible advice in hindsight. If the book had instead suggested investing in the *global* stock market, the next 23 years would have been much brighter. If that investor had just bought a global index fund, she'd have earned a positive 326 percent return instead of the 44 percent loss in the domestic Japanese portfolio.[4]

The Japanese market's two lost decades in the '90s and '00s were devastating, but other countries have suffered far worse. Between 1900 and 1948, the German stock market was a disaster, down 92 percent overall and losing almost all of its value on two separate occasions. First, following World War I, Germany dealt with hyperinflation. We've had moderate inflation in the United States since Nixon closed the gold window, but nothing like the German hyperinflation in the 1920s. In 1922, German prices rose by 742,574 percent in just 16 months, rendering the German mark worthless. One apocryphal story describes a worker who brought a wheelbarrow full of marks to buy a loaf of bread, but after going inside to see if there was any bread available, he returned to find the money dumped on the ground and the wheelbarrow stolen.[5] By 1925, the German market was down 82 percent in real terms.

The German market faced ruin again following World War II. After the Allies dismantled the three major German banks that had cooperated with the Nazis, the German stock market ceased to function. It was not until after 1948—by which time the German people had lost their savings—that a new stock market was born.[6] Again, a global focus would have sidestepped the German market disaster. During the same 48-year period, 14 of 19 major country stock markets had positive real returns and the average return across these 19 countries (between 1900 and 1948) was a positive 918 percent.[7] Italy, Japan, Austria, France, and Belgium also suffered negative returns—mostly as a result of World War II—but most markets performed very well. It would have been almost impossible for an investor to diversify across all of these countries early in the twentieth century, but today, investing in a single index fund, or exchange traded fund (ETF), you can now buy stocks in 45 countries with the click of a button. The Japanese and German examples are extreme, but they reveal the risks of concentrating your portfolio in your home country or in any one country.

The US stock market has had a remarkable multicentury run, but history tries to teach us the same lesson over and over again: countries—like companies—rise, flourish, and fade. You should heed this lesson. To think that any country or company will sustain dominance forever is naive, and for young investors, dangerous. We tend to view foreign investments as riskier than domestic ones, often for the simple reason that we are more familiar with companies where we are born and raised. There is no telling which countries or global regions will dominate in the future; as Warren Buffett reminds us, "If past history was all there was to the game, the richest people would be librarians."[8] But even when certain countries or regions lag, the overall global market has always done well. The stock market works so well because it allows investors to ride the wave of creative destruction, to take advantage of opportunities as they rise rather than hold on to failing companies as they fall. This idea can be extended to countries, and to ride the global wave of innovation and growth you need to have a global portfolio. Putting all your proverbial eggs in one basket makes no sense. You need to spread your bets.

America! Fuck Yea?

There is nothing more American than beer and burgers. Budweiser cans are emblazoned with the American flag and the brand is a staple on Super Bowl Sunday and on the Fourth of July. Burger King sells several hundred million Whoppers every year. But Budweiser is owned by Anheuser-Busch InBev, a Belgian company, and the majority owner of Burger King is 3G, a private Brazilian group. We love American companies, but globalization is blurring economic lines. Americans have a bias toward all things American, and our national pride extends into our portfolio allocations. In 2010, US investors had 72 percent of their money in US stocks even though US companies made up 43 percent of the global stock market. This imbalance—or portfolio patriotism—is not just an American phenomenon; where investors are born tends to influence what they own. Investors in the United Kingdom had a 50 percent allocation to UK stocks in 2010, even though UK stocks represented 8.6 percent of the global market.[9]

Investors everywhere prefer to own companies that are domiciled in their home country; everywhere, people are comfortable with the familiar and uncomfortable with the unknown. But portfolio patriotism too often causes us to neglect opportunities to invest in international companies that can be much better investments than domestic options. Our goal is to own good companies at great prices, so why would we limit ourselves to stocks in our home countries? While patriotism and familiarity incline us to buy local, companies around the world have trended in the opposite direction. In 2012, companies in the American S&P 500 earned 46.6 percent of their revenues outside the United States. Companies are always looking to expand their businesses and have realized that the new opportunities lie in foreign markets. To capture these opportunities, they have worked hard to grow their presence in Europe, Asia, and in the emerging markets of Africa and South America. Coca-Cola, one of our most iconic brands, is a global company, not an American one: in 2012, 65 percent of its sales were in countries outside North America.

American companies have done well since the Great Recession of 2007–2009 because they continue to succeed by innovating and looking for global opportunities. Innovation has long been the driver of American excellence and success. New technologies resulting from constant investment in research and development allow companies to stay ahead of the curve and offer new products to satisfy an evolving market. The United States continues to be a leader in innovation, but the playing field has leveled. In the 2013 Global Innovation Rankings—published by Cornell University,

INSEAD, and the World Intellectual Property Organization— Switzerland, Sweden, the United Kingdom, and the Netherlands all earned a higher score for innovation than the United States, and Hong Kong and Singapore were nipping at our heels. As the battle between Samsung and Apple for smart phone dominance has revealed, the competitive landscape has gone global. No one cares if their phone was designed and manufactured in Korea; they just want the best phone that their money can buy.

In the United States, as its debts have grown steadily, its spending on research and development has slowed; so much so that it will have a negative real growth rate in research spending in 2013. While its spending slows, research spending is booming in Asia, led by China, Japan, and South Korea. For decades the United States dominated research spending, and still spends the most of any country in raw dollars—but China has been growing its research spending by more than 10 percent a year for a decade, and Japan and South Korea now spend more on research per capita than does the United States.[10] Because the innovation race has become more competitive, we cannot expect the United States to outrun the rest of the world.

In dollar value, the United States still represents half of the global stock market, so US stocks can and should still make up a significant portion of your portfolio. But there are many foreign companies that can and should be considered; particularly when they are cheaper than their US competitors, which is often the case.

Maximizing Our Global Purchasing Power

Another advantage of investing abroad is that owning foreign companies gives you exposure to foreign currencies. If you were only going to buy local goods and services, inflation would be your primary concern, but because the United States trades so much with the outside world, the value of your local currency relative to other currencies is also important to consider. If, for example, you go on your honeymoon in Europe or buy a German car, the exchange rate between dollars and euros will play a big role in how lavish a vacation you can afford, or whether you can buy a BMW instead of a Ford Focus. If the exchange rate is one dollar for one euro, you'll be able to afford more European goods and services than if you had to exchange $1.50 for every euro.

Foreign investments provide protection against a weakening local currency because when you invest in a foreign stock you earn two kinds of returns. First, the return of that stock in its local market and, second, the return of the company's home currency versus the US dollar. For example, if you purchase stock in the South Korean company Samsung, you will earn the return of that stock as it performs in South Korean won (the return a Korean investor would earn), but you will also earn a return that reflects any changes in the exchange rate between the US dollar and the South Korean won. Let's say that Samsung stock rises by 10 percent one year on the South Korean stock exchange and, in the same year, the South Korean won strengthens against the US dollar, appreciating by 5 percent. In this case, a US investor in Samsung would earn the 10 percent return but also *benefit* from the US dollar weakening by 5 percent, earning a total return of roughly 15 percent.[11] Buying foreign stocks is like buying an insurance policy on the strength (or lack thereof) of the US dollar or other local currency.

The reverse is also true, so a strengthening of your local currency would reduce the return earned on foreign investments. But since your earnings and savings are denominated in your home currency, you already have a built-in bet on the strength of your currency. Spreading your money around to different countries a smart way to protect yourself from a potentially weak dollar. see how this can affect your investment returns, let's consider the historical returns of a global stock index for a US investor in two different ways. If you measure returns for the global stock market since 1970 in terms of the local foreign currencies where the stocks in the market trade—think of the 10 percent Samsung return above—then the total return between 1970 and June 2013 was 3,632 percent. But if you measure the return in US dollars, taking into account the currency effect and the effect of a weakening US dollar—similar to the 5 percent return above—then the total return was 5,065 percent over the same period.[12] For the US investor, the fact that the US dollar has tended to grow weaker relative to other global currencies over this period has had a positive effect on returns earned through investments in global stocks.

A Bigger Pond

Investing in the global market reduces country and currency risk, but it also makes more sense because the global market is a much larger opportunity set than any single country market. In the most prominent global stock market index, the MSCI All Country World Index, just 25 percent of the stocks are domiciled in the United States. The remaining 75 percent are diverse companies from all around the world, often trading at discounts to US stocks. You can easily buy tons of foreign companies here in the United States. There are more than 600 international stocks that we can trade with ease here on stock exchanges in the United States from 45 countries, from Taiwan to Turkey, Israel to Ireland.[13] Companies like Charles Schwab are also pioneering services that will allow individual investors to buy more foreign stocks—further reducing barriers to international investment. There are thousands of additional stocks that will become easier to purchase and own in the coming years.

Broader choices offer broader opportunities. Limiting yourself to one country is like limiting yourself to investing in one industry. Why would you own only energy stocks when there are so many other great companies in the technology, industrial, materials, and consumer industries? The same is true of global opportunities, and global investing allows us to fish in a much bigger pond.

Easy Access

In their eye-opening book *Triumph of the Optimists: 101 Years of Global Investment Returns*, authors Elroy Dimson, Paul Marsh, and Mike Staunton explain that for most of the twentieth century, access to international markets was difficult. Because buying international stocks was such a hassle, international diversification was not worth it. Often, there were country-imposed restrictions on the flow of money between countries, constraints on holding foreign stocks, and few index funds representing a global portfolio. We are fortunate because these obstacles have all but disappeared, and a large majority of large international companies can now be purchased on US stock exchanges. It is just as easy to buy AstraZeneca, a British pharmaceutical company, as it is to buy Pfizer, an American one. As the authors of *Triumph of the Optimists* point out, even with our own market doing so well, international diversification has been a boon to US investors because foreign investments have reduced our overall risk.

I'll discuss how to buy specific stocks from the market in chapter 6, but for young investors who prefer an even simpler solution, there are countless ETFs which invest in lots of different stocks like a mutual fund, but trade like an individual stock and index mutual funds, which allow us to gain instant access to global markets. Look for products that track the MSCI All Country World Index as a starting point, and explore regional options from there.

The bottom line is that global investing should be the norm. Our built-in bias toward local stocks limits our opportunities, concentrates our risk, and fails to protect us against a falling dollar or other home currency. When you go global, you can reduce your risk *and* improve your returns. It is a win-win decision.

I am thrilled that I was born in 1985 rather than 1960 because I've witnessed a remarkable shift in global relationships. As our generation has grown up, barriers between nations—both physical and figurative—have fallen. The continued integration between countries and markets creates exciting opportunities, and we are lucky to have the ability to own the global businesses that benefit from these opportunities. As innovation and business continue to go global, it won't matter where companies are headquartered. What will matter is how they take advantage of a global marketplace. We are the first generation to have such easy access to global companies, so you should position yourself so that your portfolio can grow with the world. A more global world requires a more global portfolio.

5

BE DIFFERENT

I was 22 when I started my career in money management, and my timing could not have been worse. Within 15 months of my July 3, 2007, start date, we were in crisis mode, facing one of the largest market crashes and recessions in history. The company I work for manages portfolios that are fully invested in the stock market—one of the worst places for your money in 2008—so we had many very difficult conversations with our clients. The portfolios that we manage are also very different from the overall market, so our performance can be very different as well. While we expect to outperform the market over the long term, we have periods of short-term underperformance that are painful to live through. In 2008 and 2009, my company faced a perfect storm, because, while the overall market crashed by 50 percent, several of our strategies performed even *worse*—one of our flagship strategies was down 60 percent.[1]

In one memorable meeting, following a period of bad performance for the portfolio that I was there to discuss, the financial adviser (our client) sitting opposite me refused to look me in the eye. Instead of speaking to me, he asked my colleague what a "limp dick little asshole" like myself was doing in his office. I was 23 years old, inexperienced with intense confrontation, and better equipped to discuss Notre Dame football than the stock market. Suffice it to say we didn't win any additional business from that adviser, and I left the meeting questioning my career choice.

From this meeting and several other difficult ones, I learned that being different is hard when things aren't going your way. Many clients fired us after our poor performance in 2008 and 2009, afraid that our unique portfolios would continue to lag the market. Every strategy that beats the market over the long term will have brutal periods like the one we experienced during the financial crisis. But our commitment to the strategy, even when it was lagging the market, has paid off. Between the market bottom in 2009 and the end of 2013, the flagship strategy had a positive return of 347 percent, much better than the market's 179 percent return.[2]

Many other managers had a similar experience. Bill Miller, a famous modern investor, knows a lot about being different. Miller rose to fame following an impressive and improbable winning streak. His concentrated, unique mutual fund beat the S&P 500 for 15 straight calendar years between 1991 and 2005. Thanks to his fame and outstanding track record, the Legg Mason Value Trust that he managed grew to $16.5 billion in assets. Then in 2008, his two funds collapsed; the Value Trust fund was down 55 percent and his other fund, the Legg Mason Opportunity Fund, was down 65 percent. In an already bad year, both funds did much worse than the S&P 500, which was down 37 percent in 2008. Despite his long-term success, clients fled Miller's fund—it dropped from $16.5 billion to $4 billion in assets. Being different can be hard—as it was for Miller in 2008—but it can also lead to impressive market-beating results. Since the Opportunity Fund's calamitous performance in 2008, it is up 223 percent, almost 100 percent better than the market's 128 percent return.[3]

This chapter explores how being different can lead to such exceptional results. In this chapter and the next, success is measured differently than in previous chapters. Up to this point I've discussed "absolute" and "real" returns. Absolute just means the percentage your portfolio is up or down, and real means the percentage after inflation. We will shift now to a focus on "relative" or "excess" returns, meaning the percentage by which a strategy beats or trails the overall market. For example, if your portfolio was up 15 percent last year, and the market was up 10 percent, then your portfolio had an absolute return of plus 15 percent and a relative return of plus 5 percent. If your portfolio was up 5 percent last year, then you'd still have a positive absolute return (plus 5 percent), but your excess return would be minus 5 percent because you would have lost relative to the market. Being different is worth it only if you can earn high excess returns, so your goal is to find strategies that beat the market by the greatest amount.

As a millennial investor, you can narrow your choices for investing in the stock market down to three broad categories: market indexes, alternative or "smart" indexes, and individual stocks. This chapter examines the first two in detail, leaving the individual stock category for chapter 6. What we will learn is that while market-index mutual funds and ETFs are a good starting point, you should buy smart index funds and ETFs whenever possible. History teaches us that the more you differentiate your portfolio from the market, the better your chances to beat the market—and smart index strategies are a great first step on the quest to be different. To understand why, we must first understand the thing from which we are trying to be different: the market index.

Mr. Market

Whenever someone refers to "the market," they mean an index that tracks stocks in a specific category or geographic area. There are indexes for US stocks, for the emerging markets, for European stocks, and countless others to choose from. The most common markets in the United States are the S&P 500, which includes 500 of the largest American companies, and the Dow Jones Industrial Average, which includes 30 companies and is the oldest market index, established in 1896 by Charles Dow. If you turn on the nightly news, you will learn how the S&P 500 or Dow performed that day. For the reasons laid out earlier, *global* indexes are the better choice for modern investors, and therefore the MSCI All Country World Index is the best index to measure the market today, because it includes major companies from 45 countries around the world.

Regardless of which index we are referring to, the market that we choose to follow is important because it helps us evaluate our success or failure as investors. Money managers get hired because they have beaten the market, and they get fired when the market is beating them. I learned early in my career that being different means that a company's clients will vacillate between thinking its money managers are geniuses or morons, and it all depends on how their portfolios performed in the recent past.

Because market indexes are our benchmarks for success or failure, it is important to understand how they are built—and where their weaknesses lie. Market indexes are defined by one characteristic: size. How big each company is (in terms of its market value) determines how much it influences the index's returns. For simplicity sake, let's pretend that the global market is worth $100 in total, and that Apple, Inc. is worth five dollars. In this scenario,

Apple would represent 5 percent of the global market index, and therefore have a huge impact on that index's returns. If Samsung is worth one dollar, it too will have an important impact on returns, but only one-fifth the impact Apple does. Furthermore, as companies grow, their weight in the index also grows. If you own an index fund, your returns will be determined most by the performance of the world's largest stocks.[4]

Indexes like the S&P 500 and the MSCI All Country World Index have been around a long time, but index *funds* have just recently gained popularity. In reality, an index is just a list of stocks and weights that are proportional to the size of each company; an index is a portfolio on paper. Indexes were designed to track the market's overall performance—much like GDP growth tracks the economy's performance. Investing changed forever when the first index mutual fund was launched in 1976. An index fund seeks to match the return of the paper index by buying all the same stocks in the same quantities as the paper portfolio. Index funds were so revolutionary because they allowed any investor to gain access to a huge group of companies for a very low fee. These index funds (and now index ETFs) are managed to replicate their respective index's returns; they never try to beat the market, they just try to match the returns of the paper portfolio.

The Case for Index Investing

Index funds have been great for the industry and they have grown more popular for good reasons. But after exploring why index funds are a good option, we will see that we can do better. Twenty years ago, in 1993, index funds had a 3.2 percent market share, but by 2012, that share had risen to 17.4 percent, and today more than

$1 trillion is invested in stock market index products.[5] Because they provided low-cost access to entire markets, index mutual funds were revolutionary for baby boomers. With index funds, boomers never had to worry about losing to the market, because they could match its return with ease.

Index funds will likely continue to win market share, because millennials are happy to just earn the market rate of return. In a 2014 survey, when asked "which of the following best describes your investment approach," only 17 percent of millennial respondents said that their goal was to outperform the market. Other respondents were happy to just earn the market's rate of return (36 percent of respondents), were fine earning low returns so long as they had downside protection (23 percent), or were more concerned with personal goals than with the market's return (24 percent).[6] Index funds are popular with young investors for two very compelling reasons. The first is that they are dirt cheap. You will typically pay between 0.09 percent and 0.2 percent of your account value per year to own these products—an amazing bargain. If you had $100,000 invested in the S&P 500 (using the exchange traded fund SPY), you'd only pay $90 per year in fees. Because their fees are so low and they are so easy to buy, index funds have torn down the barriers to investing in the global stock market. These low fees have been good for investors because they have brought down management fees across the board—a trend that will continue to benefit millennial investors; lower fees translate into better returns.

The second compelling reason to own index funds is that despite their simple and passive investment strategy (i.e., buy big stocks—the bigger the better), they tend to outperform other options. Most people interested in investing want to beat the market, but individuals and professional investors alike have a very hard time doing so. Investors that do consistently beat the market are the exception rather than the rule. I will explore investor underperformance in detail when we get to part three of our investing formula: "get out of your own way." But for now, the important point is that even professionally managed mutual funds have a hard time beating the market. Historically, just 30 percent of mutual funds have beaten the market in rolling ten-year periods.[7] Trying to pick which funds will be in the 30 percent in the *next* ten years is very hard to do. In the most recent five-year periods (through 2012), the results were even worse: just 25 percent of large capitalization mutual funds beat the S&P 500 after fees, and just 10 percent of medium capitalization (aka mid-cap) mutual funds beat the S&P MidCap 400 index after fees.[8] A big reason for this putrid performance record is that many professional investors have lacked consistency and discipline, and they charge higher fees. Both problems erode returns for their investors over time. In the latest five-year period (again through 2012), managers have been very inconsistent—the majority (53 percent) of mutual funds switched styles during this period.[9] Switching styles can be dangerous, and switching at the right time is difficult.

An index like the S&P 500 is built based on basic rules that do not change, so an index is always consistent and, in its own way, always disciplined. Because it is so hard to beat these basic indexes, many successful market thinkers continue to believe that the stock market is "efficient," meaning that current stock prices are exactly what they should be, and trying to guess otherwise by owning unique portfolios is a fool's errand. If the market were indeed efficient, then there would be no edge for investors interested in beating the market and the rest of this book would be a waste of your time. If the market were efficient, then index funds would be the only logical choice.

I will admit that the weak fund performance described above is disheartening, but there is an upside to the rise of index investing. With more and more investors thinking that it is impossible to beat the market, there is more opportunity for those seeking an edge. As Warren Buffett asked in his annual letter to shareholders in 1985, "What could be more advantageous in an intellectual contest—whether it be bridge, chess or stock selection—than to have opponents who have been taught that thinking is a waste of energy." The idea that markets are efficient remains very popular. Almost 30 years after Buffet's clever observation, one of the intellectual leaders of the efficient-market movement, Eugene Fama, was awarded the 2013 Nobel Prize in economic sciences.[10] Record index fund sales prove that many market participants have resigned themselves to the idea "if you can't beat 'em, join 'em." I view this as a positive, because less competition is a good thing for investors who want to beat the market. The bottom line is that index funds have improved investing in every way: they allow easier access to global markets and they lead to lower overall fees and less competition for those of us trying to beat the index. But like Achilles, index investing has its own vulnerable heel.

Follow the Leader?

The primary weakness of market index products is that they have the investment strategy backward. Owning more of a company just because it is bigger than others is a bone-headed way to build a portfolio. Even stupid strategies can beat a market-capitalization-weighted index. If you bought all large stocks in the United States that started with the letter C, you'd have outperformed the S&P 500 by 0.5 percent per year since 1962.[11] This works because the C strategy does not have a bias toward the largest stocks. I hope it strikes you as odd that this random sample of companies can beat a market-cap-weighted index, yet index funds are gaining market share every year. I doubt any investors would buy an index called "The Letter C 500," but if one existed it might be a better option than the S&P 500. The trouble with the index strategy is that the largest stocks tend to underperform after they've reached the top. To understand how and why, let's investigate two simple investment strategies called Sector Leaders and Sector Bargains. Even though they are less well-known, the Sector Bargains deliver much better returns.

If you had to pick between two baseball teams, would you rather have a team of players with the highest salaries in the league or a team of players with the highest performance statistics like on-base percentage, lowest earned-run averages, and fewest defensive errors? The highest-paid players have all had exceptional careers and as a result they have commanded the highest prices on the free-agent market. But a high payroll doesn't guarantee success: since 2000, only 5 of 13 Major League Baseball championship teams have had a *top-five* payroll during their championship year (the Yankees twice and the Red Sox three times). Investing in index funds is similar to opting for a team with the highest-paid superstars. The largest companies have excelled in the past just like the highest-paid players, but these companies tend to underperform other companies after reaching the top.

This brings us to the first investment strategy, Sector Leaders. Much like an index, this strategy buys stocks based on their size. It is an easy strategy to test—every year since 1962 this strategy buys the largest US stock by its total value (market capitalization) in each of the ten major economic sectors: industrials, consumer staples, consumer discretionary, energy, materials, telecommunications, information technology, utilities, financials, and health care. Each of the ten stocks then represents 10 percent of the portfolio, and the stocks and percentage weights are updated annually. I am focusing on the US market to start so that the companies are recognizable and because we have much longer term data for US stocks than for international stocks, but we will see later that the same story applies to the global market.

In January 2014, the sector leaders were Amazon.com, Apple, AT&T, ExxonMobil, General Electric, Johnson & Johnson, Procter & Gamble, Monsanto Company, Duke Energy Corporation, and Wells Fargo—all market champions and titans of our economy. These ten stocks alone represent 15 percent of the S&P 500, a remarkable weight given that there are 500 companies in the index. If you were to buy an S&P 500 index fund, therefore, these companies would have a huge impact on your performance during any given year.

These companies are well-known and successful, so having them as the cornerstone of your portfolio may be enticing. But the amazing thing about the sector leaders is that they have underperformed the overall market since 1962. They have produced a 9.1 percent annual return, which is 1 percent lower per year than the S&P 500's average annual return. One percent per year may not sound like much, but it adds up over time. Since 1962, the S&P 500 has grown by 12,500 percent but the Sector Leaders strategy has grown by a much smaller 8,100 percent—a 4,400 percent difference in total return that could mean millions of dollars to a long-term portfolio. Thanks to the power of compounding, 1 percent per year can have a tremendous snowball effect. This strategy shows that investing a large chunk of one's portfolio in the largest stocks has been a drag on returns.

There are several reasons the Sector Leaders strategy loses compared to the overall market. First, it is very hard for leading companies to stay on top. When you are the leader in your industry, countless other smaller companies are working hard to steal your business and reduce your market share by offering better and/or cheaper products. Second, while the Sector Leaders have done well thanks to skilled employees and market-leading products or services, there is always luck involved in any success story, and luck evens out over time. In markets—and in sports, business, and life in general—there is a powerful force called reversion to the mean. The tendency for things to return to normal helps explain the Madden and *Sports Illustrated* curses, where athletes tend to disappoint after they appear on the cover of a major video game or sports magazine. These athletes make it onto the covers because they've been the best at what they do in the past month or past year, but after rising to the top they tend to then revert to more average performance levels. Companies at the top have made it there thanks to hard work—and luck. While General Electric and ExxonMobil have led the industrial and energy sectors (respectively) since 1962, the remaining eight sectors have had an average of eight different leaders over the same time period. Leadership shifts, and in the future old companies will lose their edge and new exciting companies will rise to the top.

The Sector Leaders strategy illustrates the problem for young investors buying index funds or ETFs: they place too much weight in several key stocks at the top of the heap—stocks that have had a great run, but tend to fall back to earth after reaching the top. Only six American companies have ever been worth $400 billion: Cisco, General Electric, Intel, ExxonMobil, Apple, and Microsoft. They all first hit that threshold between 1999 and 2012, but since hitting the threshold, they've had a negative annual return on average. Of the six, only Apple and ExxonMobil have had positive returns. Size is often a major headwind for stock returns, and yet size is the main criteria determining how much of a stock will be purchased in an index fund or ETF.

Sector Bargains

If instead of buying the biggest companies, you buy the *cheapest*, then you can build a portfolio that crushes the market. This strategy, called Sector Bargains, will serve as an introduction to our second investing category: alternative, or smart, index products. Returning to the baseball analogy, many readers will be familiar with the classic book (and movie) *Moneyball* by Michael Lewis about the revolutionary method for finding the best baseball players using various player statistics. The method, designed by Bill James and employed by Oakland A's general manager Billy Beane, identifies players who may be diamonds in the rough by focusing on statistics like how often the player gets on base (on-base percentage). For the Oakland A's, this method was ideal because the A's didn't have an unlimited payroll like the Yankees or the Red Sox; they had to pay special attention to the price for each player. Their strategy was to find players with good statistics for a good price. The Sector Bargains strategy follows a similar approach: it searches large stocks in the same ten economic sectors already mentioned, but instead of buying the biggest stock from each sector, it buys the cheapest.

The list of companies in the Sector Bargains strategy is never as exciting as the list in the Sector Leaders strategy; these companies tend to fly under the radar. If they are in the news, it is often for the wrong reasons, like poor recent earnings, changes in leadership, or a declining competitive advantage. Ever heard of CF Industries? Computer Sciences Corporation? Entergy Corporation? These are three of the ten companies in the Sector Bargains strategy in January 2014, and while they may not inspire, they are dirt cheap.

Stocks trading at discount prices have provided investors with a huge edge.

You must pay special attention to the price that you are paying for any stock, because the less you pay, the more you will earn from your investments. In the stock market, price is a sign of expectations. The higher the price relative to sales, profits (earnings), and other fundamentals, the more investors expect from that company for the future. The Sector Bargains strategy buys stocks for which the market has much lower expectations. Lucky for you, these expectations are often *too* low, meaning there is a big potential upside in the stock. The Oakland A's shocked the baseball world when they amassed a 20-game win streak—a league record—with the third smallest payroll in the league. Investing in robust but unloved players worked wonders for the A's, and the same strategy works for stocks.

There are many ways to measure how cheap a stock is, but the easiest method is to compare annual results for the company (profits, sales, cash flows) to its current market price. Investors should pay as little as possible for every dollar of profits or sales a company is producing. If each year you bought the cheapest company in each sector—selected from the same large stock universe that I used for the Sector Leaders strategy—then your annual return would have been 15.9 percent per year since 1962, a massive improvement over the 9.1 percent earned in the Sector Leaders strategy.[12] If your investment horizon was 30 years, the power of compounding gives you an enormous edge. In the average 30-year period, a $10,000 investment in the Sector Leaders strategy would have grown to $136,000, but an investment in the Sector Bargains strategy would have grown to more than $830,000.

One way to take advantage of value investing is to look for smart or alternative indexes that have "value" in their name.

A value index, such as the Russell 1000 Value, named for founder Frank Russell, selects stocks based on their cheapness. Because cheap stocks outperform the market over time, value indexes represent an incremental improvement over normal indexes, like the S&P 500, that are based solely on size. They won't have results as dramatic as those in the Sector Bargains because they will not be as concentrated as my ten-stock strategy, but chances are high that they will beat size-weighted market indexes over time. These value indexes have been around a long time, and have proven themselves to be a superior option for investors. The longest running value index is the Russell 3000 Value, which owns a wide variety of US stocks that are cheaper than other stocks in the market. Investors can buy the Russell 3000 Value using either an ETF or a mutual fund. Since January 1979, the Russell 3000 Value index has outperformed the S&P 500 by more than 1,100 percent.[13] In the stock market, buying cheap stocks is a powerful way to earn massive returns.

The difference in annual returns between the Sector Leaders and the Sector Bargains strategy in the United States is large, but the difference is even more extreme for the *global* Sector Leaders and Sector Bargains. Between January 1990 and June 2013, the global Sector Leaders strategy had an annual return of just 4.75 percent, while the global Sector Bargains had an annual return of 21 percent per year! This huge gap is the result of a bigger opportunity set—several cheap companies around the globe had remarkable returns during this period, and the Sector Bargains strategy took full advantage of them. The global Sector Leaders had such a low return because of several Japanese stocks which performed poorly, like Tokyo Power and Electric and Nippon Telegraph and Telephone. These two were the global leaders in the utility and telecommunications sectors for a large portion of the last 23 years, but both stocks have had *negative* total returns since 1990. The great returns from the global Sector Bargains strategy are just one more reason why going global is so important for millennial investors.

The Millennial Edge

Buying cheap stocks is one way to beat the market, but there are several other ways that also work well. Strategies based on market momentum, shareholder orientation, earnings quality, and low volatility have all delivered strong relative returns. Using these alternative characteristics to build simple ten-stock sector strategies like Sector Leaders and Sector Bargains, you'd have earned annual returns of 14.2 percent (Sector Winners—market momentum), 14.7 percent (Sector Stewards—shareholder orientation), 12.1 percent (Sector Stalwarts—earnings quality), and 11.5 percent (Sector Steadies—low volatility). Each strategy has easily trumped the Sector Leaders (9.1 percent) and the S&P 500 (10.0 percent).

Here is a brief description of each, along with average 30-year outperformance versus the S&P 500.[14] I've also included the keyword (italicized) to look for when searching for smart indexes built using similar criteria. Each strategy has a one-year holding period before re-evaluating and rebalancing.[15]

Sector Winners (average 30-year outperformance of 3,600 percent).   Newton's first law of motion says that objects in motion remain in motion unless acted on by an outside force. This law has an investing equivalent, because stocks in motion tend to remain in motion, too. This strategy buys the stock in each sector with the best *momentum* over the previous year.[16]

Sector Stewards (average 30-year outperformance of 4,400 percent).   Companies have two ways to return cash to shareholders. They can pay a regular dividend (one to four times per year) or they can repurchase stock from shareholders. When you buy shares of a company, you are placing your money in the hands of the company's managers. These managers are stewards of your money, and the best stewards are those that send cash back to their shareholders. Companies with good shareholder orientation have performed very well historically, as evidenced by the massive average outperformance for the Sector Stewards over 30-year investment periods. This strategy buys the stock from each of the ten sectors with the highest *shareholder yield* that has returned the most cash to shareholders through both dividend and share-repurchase programs.[17]

Sector Steadies (average 30-year outperformance of 850 percent). One simple and popular way to select stocks is based on their market volatility. Stocks that have been less volatile than their peers outperform the market and do so with less volatility. The amazing thing about this strategy is that, like the Sector Winners strategy, it is based only on market movement. It is not as powerful as the Sector Bargains strategy, but it has still provided market-beating results. Low-volatility strategies are great for investors worried about risk, because they do very well in markets that are crashing. For example, the Sector Steadies were down 37 percent between November 2008 and February 2009, during which time the S&P 500 was down 51 percent. This strategy buys the stock from each of the ten sectors that has the *lowest volatility* over the past year.[18]

Sector Stalwarts (average 30-year outperformance of 1,390 percent). The long-term goal for any company is to earn significant profits, which it can use to reinvest or pay out to shareholders. But profits vary in quality; they can come from real cash flows, or they can be "created" by corporate managers to make quarterly reports look better than they really are (think Enron). I will explore this topic in much more detail in chapter 6, but the short version is that cash flow is king, and companies with strong cash flows outperform the market. This strategy buys stocks in each of the ten sectors with the highest *quality* earnings.[19]

If anything, these strategies are *too simple,* but they make the point that it is very easy to beat the market with the right strategy. While the next chapter will explore the power of combining these ideas into a single market-beating strategy, it is important to understand how powerful single-factor strategies like these sector strategies can be, because most smart index strategies currently available focus on one factor, like low volatility or high momentum. These smart indexes are run just like the indexes that track the overall market, but instead of using size as the key factor, they use cheapness, quality, market momentum, and other criteria that I have introduced here. These strategies work because they have the same discipline and consistency as a normal index, but a much smarter method to choose stocks.

✳   ✳   ✳

Index investing was the key development for our parents' generation, and alternative, smart index strategies will be the key development for the millennial generation. We are still in the early days of smarter indexing, but new products are launching all the time. As they continue to outperform traditional indexes, they should become available in retirement-account platforms. For now, we should invest in the best products available in our retirement accounts and buy smart indexes in our normal investment accounts. Chapter 10 provides a complete hierarchy of the best investment options for either account.

Along with our long-term horizon, access to better strategies is the largest edge that we have as an investing generation. If we invest in smarter indexes, we can earn more impressive returns than those from traditional indexes. If we were to expand our time horizon to 40 years and the Sector Leaders and Sector Bargains strategies earn a similar return as they have in the past, then a $10,000 investment in Sector Leaders would grow to $325,000, but the same $10,000 investment in Sector Bargains would grow to $3,660,000. A smarter strategy used over a long time period is a powerful combination, and we can exploit this chemistry to grow rich.

The Power of Being Different

If you are evaluating different investment options—be they mutual funds, ETFs, or something else—opt for those that are the most different from the market, because they have the best chance to outperform. To measure just how different any portfolio is from the market, we can give the portfolio a score between 1 and 100, where a perfect score of 100 would mean that the portfolio is *completely* different from a market index like the S&P 500. Scoring a perfect 100 would be very hard to do because it would mean you don't own a single stock out of the 500 stocks in the index. Most portfolios have some overlap with the market, but a score above 80 or 90 would still mean that you are *very* different. Two researchers, Martijn Cremers and Antti Petajisto, have investigated what such a score means for mutual fund returns, and found that the higher a mutual fund's score, the better its returns. They call this score between 1 and 100 "active share," because it describes the percentage of a portfolio that is unique or different from the index. A strategy like Sector Bargains has an active share above 90, because more than 90 percent is different than the index.

In their study Cremers and Petajisto found that the average mutual fund lost to the market by an average of minus 0.43 percent per year, after subtracting fees. But when they separated the funds into five groups based on their active-share score, they uncovered a very interesting trend. Funds that fall in the group with the highest active share (with the most different portfolios) have outperformed their benchmark by 2.4 percent per year before fees and by 1.13 percent after fees.[20] So even though the average fund was a loser, the funds that were the most different were winners relative to the market. The sector strategies work in part because the resulting portfolios are very different from the broad market. Of course, there are ways that being different can also be very stupid. You could own the ten most expensive stocks instead of the ten cheapest and you'd have a very different—but disastrous—portfolio. Buying the most expensive stock from each sector would have been a terrible strategy in the past: delivering a 3.6 percent annual return, more than 6 percent lower per year than the 10 percent return for the S&P 500. Being different is key, but doing so in a smart, proven way is even better.

A key lesson from the study is that if you want to beat the market, you should invest in portfolios that are different from the market with higher active-share scores. If a strategy has a low score, you may as well buy a cheaper index fund.

So why doesn't everyone embrace portfolios that are different from the market? The main reason is that while you will outperform in the long term using strategies like Sector Bargains, you will have to endure short-term periods when you are losing relative to the overall market. For many investors, these short-term periods are too emotionally difficult to endure. The Sector

Bargains strategy does well over time, but it loses to the market 30 percent of the time in one-year periods, and 12 percent of the time in three-year periods. There was even one three-year period when the Sector Bargains lost by 30 percent. Money managers have gotten fired for much less. Thinking back to the early days of my career, it was very hard to explain poor recent performance to clients—sticking with any strategy through tough times will always be challenging. These short time frames should not matter to long-term investors, but humans focus on the short term, so these periods can be difficult to live through. Three years feels like an eternity when you are losing, so strong resolve and discipline are required. While smart strategies will sometimes make you feel dumb, the results they have delivered over the long-term make them well worth the effort.

Picking Stocks

Having explored index investing and smart index investing, we turn now to the final option: buying concentrated portfolios of individual stocks. This option is the most interesting and the most temping, and offers the best chance to earn unique returns—good and bad—relative to the market. The most famous and revered investors fall into this category, and they have achieved rock star status because they buy stocks that crush the market.

One of the common characteristics of smart index products is that they spread their bets across hundreds of different stocks so as to be very well diversified across industries, geographies, and/or currencies. Buying individual stocks results in much more concentrated portfolios with between ten and 100 holdings. These portfolios have very high "active shares," so they provide the best chance for huge excess returns, but also the highest likelihood of ruin.

The Sector Bargain strategy is one example of a very concentrated portfolio—just ten stocks—that offers huge excess return. For those that want to directly control their investments, building your own portfolios can be very rewarding.

The key to picking stocks is to find a great investment strategy and then stick to it through whatever the market throws at you. The sector strategies are fine examples of different styles of investing. The individual styles used for each strategy are the most famous and successful styles that we have uncovered by studying market history, but there are other styles that work well, too. In the next chapter, I will describe my personal research journey, and the hybrid investment style that I feel is best. The result is a strategy with five rules that I believe will outperform even smart indexes.

The Market Is Good, but Different Is Better

Index funds, despite their one major flaw (overemphasizing large companies), are a great starting point for owning stocks. They are easy to purchase, charge very low fees, and provide essential access to the global stock market. The growth of index funds and ETFs has been a good thing for investors because it has driven down costs across the board for investment products, so investors pay less to the people managing their money. But as the sector strategies demonstrate, we can outperform the market by using smarter investment criteria to build unique portfolios.

There is an important difference between a great company and a great stock. A great stock is one that is most likely to outperform its peers *in the future*, not one that has done well in the past. Isaac Asimov could have been talking about the stock market when he said that "past glories are poor feeding." To earn impressive, market-beating returns we must ignore past glories and focus on stocks with cheap valuations, strong momentum, low volatility, strong balance sheets, and an orientation toward the interests of their shareholders. As I learned in the first years of my career, and as many famous managers have experienced in their careers, being different will be hard sometimes. But if you stick with a proven strategy, you can beat the market by significant margins in the long term. Smart strategies are a great way for millennial investors to build different portfolios, but the best possible strategy combines all of the elements discussed in this chapter. For the Millennial Money strategy presented in chapter 6, the whole is greater than the sum of its parts.

6

THE MILLENNIAL MONEY STRATEGY

The previous chapter explored why you should be different from the market by investing in alternative or smart factor-based strategies. This chapter dives deeper into being different by building an ideal, rules-based stock selection strategy. Most smart strategies invest based on one or two attributes, like value or quality, and hold hundreds of stocks. While this is a good start, you can earn even more impressive returns if you combine more attributes and use them to build a concentrated portfolio. In this chapter, I will present five rules for picking stocks, which we will combine into the Millennial Money strategy.

* * *

Most success stories boil down to two simple things: strategy and perseverance. Develop a great plan and then stick to it—always be consistent. Strategy is more interesting because it is varied, nuanced, and unique to a given goal. Perseverance and consistency are boring—you can't say much about it other than "persevere!"

I've always loved developing strategies and plans, but I've often had a hard time sticking to them. After college, I gained 35 pounds thanks to my new sedentary office lifestyle. I'd commit to slimming down, lose 15 pounds, and then gain it back during the holidays. Starting every January, I'd work out hard for a few months and then lose interest. I wanted to eat better, work out more, give back more, experiment more, and be healthier—but I was all talk and no walk. I'm sure the items on my self-help wish list look familiar to many; maybe you've even tried and failed to reform your ways as I did for years.

Fed up with failure, I decided to change my tactics and make a public "one-year pledge" to do all these things in a formal way. I built a website (oneyearpledge.com), recruited friends and family to join me, and kicked off the year. The plan was very simple: over the course of one year, I would avoid certain key foods (no exceptions), work out three times per week, take two months off drinking, experiment with something new every month, give a set amount to charity, and read a certain number of books. A month into the pledge, it became clear that I had underestimated how difficult my plan would be to put into practice. Sitting in Molly's—my favorite Irish pub in New York City—with my friends and denying myself a Guinness was brutal. Taking all that time off from drinking was restorative, but difficult (when you are drinking, nothing good happens after 1:00 a.m.; when you are sober, it's more like 9:00 p.m.). When the one-year mark was approaching, I planned on having cookies and beer for dinner to celebrate crossing the finish line. But when the night finally came, I couldn't do it. The habits had been too deeply ingrained in me and I felt too good to go back to my old ways. What the yearlong experiment taught me was perseverance. The particulars of my plan could have been modified in countless ways, yet I still would have achieved the same results. It was perseverance and consistency that made me successful.

My successes with the one-year pledge were small in scale, but similar strategies for perseverance have led to success on the grandest scale. When I was outlining the one-year pledge, I kept thinking about Jerry Seinfeld. I've always loved his comedy, but never fully appreciated his method and commitment until I read a story about how he crafts his jokes. He has always been my favorite comic because he is able to churn out hilarious observations about the world, avoid crudeness, deliver his jokes with perfect timing, and make audiences roar with laughter. His jokes are simple and brilliant, like: "Dogs are the leaders of the planet. If you see two life forms, one of them's making a poop, the other one's carrying it for him, who would you assume is in charge?" Or, "According to most studies, people's number one fear is public speaking. Number two is death. Death is number two!? Does that sound right? This means for the average person, if you go to a funeral, they'd rather be in the casket than doing the eulogy." I always assumed that Seinfeld just had a brilliant comedic mind, and that these jokes just materialized in his brain. But his success is much more complicated. He works tirelessly on all his routines, tweaking the order of words, the inflection of his voice during delivery, and so on. He never misses a day of working on his routine, and he has a simple system to ensure his continued vigilance. He simply marks a red X on his calendar any day that he works on his routine, which forms a chain of X's. To stay motivated, he vows never to break the chain of X's; and the longer the chain gets, the harder it is to break. Simple tactic, incredible results.

Every investing strategy—no matter how great—will fail without similar perseverance and consistency. There will be three- or five-year chunks of time, for example, when any strategy loses to the S&P 500 or MSCI All Country World Index and during those periods of time it will be extremely tempting to abandon it. Don't! As I will demonstrate, the Millennial Money strategy can help you build a significant fortune, but only if you stick with it.

To bridge the gap between strategy and perseverance, we turn to an element common to both: consistency. If you can just be consistent with your investment strategy, you will be better off than the majority of investors out there. Recall from chapter 5 that 53 percent of professionally managed mutual funds changed styles in just the past five years, which means that the majority of people that invest for a living had an inconsistent strategy. People, even professionals, are inconsistent by nature. For example, as psychologist Daniel Kahneman reports, when experienced radiologists are asked to evaluate an X-ray as normal or abnormal for the *second* time—after having already evaluated the slide earlier—they contradict their previous judgment 20 percent of the time.[1] Other studies of the judgments made by auditors, pathologists, and psychologists show a similar degree of inconsistency. Successful investing is all about predicting the future, but human beings make inconsistent and therefore unreliable judgments. As Kahneman says, "Unreliable judgments cannot be valid predictors of anything." For investors this is a big problem, because if we want to beat the market, then prediction is everything.

Consistency can fix a lot of problems. Atul Gawande, a surgeon and author, has explored the power of a simple checklist for improving efficiency and safety in the operating room. Surgery, like investing, is an extremely complex activity with lots of moving parts and lots of opportunities to make mistakes. In his book *The Checklist Manifest*, Gawande argues that a checklist can make us more consistent and improve our performance on complex tasks.[2] In one stunning example, Gawande describes an experiment conducted by clinical care specialist Peter Pronovost to test how a five-part checklist could decrease the infection rate in central-line-insertion procedures. The checklist he developed for doctors to use while inserting a central line into patients was straightforward: (1) wash your hands, (2) sterilize the patient's skin, (3) cover the patient in sterile drapes, (4) wear a sterile mask, hat, gown, and gloves, and (5) sterilize the insertion point once the line is in. For the first month of the experiment, Pronovost instructed nurses to observe how often doctors would skip one of these steps; they did so more than one-third of the time. In the year following the initial month of observation, the nurses were given the authority to intervene when they saw a doctor miss a step and insist that each of the five steps be followed during every procedure. As nurses intervened over the next year, the checklist resulted in a remarkable decrease in the infection rate. The rate fell from 11 percent to 0 percent—from 34 infections to none. This huge drop prevented eight deaths and saved $2 million (which would have resulted from the costs associated with infections). The study continued for an additional 15 months and there were only two infections. A little nudge toward consistency had a huge impact, all in one hospital.

Investing Checklists

The same principle works in investing, and there are many famous investors who have developed their own checklists. Benjamin Graham—father of value investing and the original investing legend—had a list that he presented in his classic book *The Intelligent Investor*, first published in 1949. Here is a simplified version of his suggested checklist for the defensive investor. A stock must have:

- ☑ A price-to-earnings ratio below 15
- ☑ A price-to-book ratio below 1.5

☑ At least twice as many short-term assets (e.g., inventories, cash) as current debts (e.g., accounts payable)

☑ Long-term debt lower than net current assets (i.e., the company could pay off its debt with its short-term capital)

☑ Profits that have grown in the past year[3]

The beauty of this list, like the checklist for safer central-line insertions, is that it is so basic. It requires you to buy companies in good financial positions that are growing but still cheap. I rebuilt Graham's checklist and identified every company that has met his criteria in every year since 1962. This modified version of Graham's famous checklist winnows a universe of thousands of companies down to an average of just 75 at any given time, and long after its origination it has continued to identify stocks that beat the market. Graham's defensive stocks have grown by 14.7 percent per year, beating the S&P 500 by an average of 4,400 percent in 30-year periods. Graham's basic ideas remain relevant more than 60 years later: having the discipline to buy good companies at cheap prices remains the best way to build a fortune in the stock market.

Ben Graham did not have the luxury of modern computers, nor the vast amounts of market data that we are fortunate to have today. While his strategy works well, there are several ways that we can improve upon it. I set out to take everything I've learned about investing and incorporate all of the best ideas into a single strategy for the millennial investor. So armed, millennials can follow in the footsteps of investing legends with a modern checklist for success.

Building my checklist took a lot of research and a lot of testing. I wanted to incorporate the best elements from several different investing styles and to distill each element down to a single factor. I considered more than 100 different ways of evaluating a stock, including two used by Graham—price-to-book ratio and price-to-earnings ratio. Once I settled on the best factors, I set up strategy tests that identify all stocks passing my checklist every month since 1962. I then built hypothetical portfolios of these stocks (which would own an equal amount of all stocks passing the checklist) and calculated their returns versus the market.

We are able to test almost any stock selection strategy across more than five decades in the United States and more than 25 years outside the United States. The ability to test strategies on historical data is both a gift and a curse. It is a gift because a test can validate or disprove an investing hypothesis (e.g., we should buy companies with great sales growth) and give investors a sense for when a strategy works and when it struggles. But the ability to test strategies with ease is also a curse because, if you do enough testing, you'll end up with a ton of strategies that have worked remarkably well in the past, but may not work in the future. As the saying goes, if you torture data long enough, it will tell you whatever you want to hear. With that in mind, it is important to build a strategy that has done well *and* makes sense. This is crucial, because plenty of things predict market returns but make zero sense. For example, if you consider butter production in Bangladesh alongside sheep population in New Zealand, you can "predict" 99 percent of the S&P 500's return between 1981 and 1993. This is a remarkably high correlation, but it doesn't mean we should buy the S&P 500 when butter production spikes.[4]

Building the Millennial Money Checklist

Ask a thousand investors what they believe is the key to beating the market and you will probably get a thousand different answers. There are many ways to outperform the market, but I've built a strategy based on five key attributes, all of which I mentioned briefly in chapter 5 and will expand on now. In the rest of this chapter, I will create a rule for each of these five attributes. As we shall see, each works well on its own, but they are even more powerful when combined together into the Millennial Money strategy. The strategy identifies companies that:

- ☑ Have shareholder friendly practices (pay dividends, buy back shares, and pay down their debt)
- ☑ Earn strong returns on *their* investments (companies invest in machines, people and research and should earn a good return on these investments)
- ☑ Have high-quality earnings (strong cash flows)
- ☑ Are cheap (attractive price versus their earnings, cash flows, etc.)
- ☑ Have improving market expectations (improving price trends)

Each rule is important, and each has helped many successful investors beat the market. Let's walk through how and why each rule works—in order—before combining them into our final checklist.

Rule #1—What's Best for Shareholders?

Up first is identifying companies with shareholder-friendly practices. Companies have several ways they can use their hard-earned cash. They can reinvest in their businesses, pay back creditors, pay shareholders, or acquire other companies. Companies can also raise cash by borrowing from creditors or by selling new stock to shareholders in the stock market. What a company chooses from this menu of options has a significant impact on the returns of its stock in the future. We can test which of these cash-spending (or money-raising) options best benefits shareholders by looking at four kinds of companies: empire builders, reckless acquirers, cash fiends, and shareholder stewards. From these examples, we can choose what type of companies to focus on in the Millennial Money strategy. Let's look at the results.

Empire Builders.   These are the 10 percent of companies that have grown their spending on things like property, buildings, or equipment (known as capital expenditures) the most over the prior year; these companies are aggressively investing in their businesses and trying to expand. This may sound like a good thing, but often these companies are overzealous with their expansion plans, and, because they are growing so quickly, the market sets an expensive price for their shares. Investors often expect high growth rates to continue, so they pay a premium for these stocks, pricing them at levels more expensive than 60 percent of stocks available, on average.[5] But history teaches us that investors are not justified in their enthusiasm for these stocks—empire builders have performed terribly relative to the market. Their annual return was just 5.4 percent, 4.6 percent lower per year than the S&P 500. If the same returns persist in the future, empire builders would lose relative to the market by more than 1,300 percent over an average 30-year period.[6]

Reckless Acquirers.   Another way for companies to spend money is to acquire other firms. Sometimes it makes sense to acquire another company—it could be a fierce competitor or have useful technology that would improve the combined business. But when a company *overpays* for another company, it is a bad sign for the future returns of its stock. Such an overpayment is recorded into an account called "goodwill." Reckless acquirers are the

10 percent of companies whose goodwill has increased by the greatest percentage in the last year. Like the empire builders, reckless acquirers have also lost to the market. They've posted an annual gain of 6.4 percent, 2.6 percent lower per year than the S&P 500. If the same returns persist in the future, reckless acquirers would lose to the market by more than 700 percent over an average 30-year period.[7]

Cash Fiends.   The next group, which have also been toxic investments, includes the top 10 percent of companies that have raised a ton of cash from creditors and new shareholders in the past year. One of the problems with selling more stock to shareholders is that, following the sale, each share represents a smaller percentage of the overall company. This means that old shareholders are seeing their holdings being diluted, which is a bad thing. Imagine two lemonade stand companies, Squeezers and Sweet-Ade, which both want to open up additional stands. Squeezers uses cash it has made from selling lemonade to slowly set up new stands. Sweet-Ade is more aggressive; it is expanding from one to five stands, but can't finance the expansion through its own earnings, so instead it borrowed some money from one friend and gave another friend a 25 percent stake in the business in exchange for more cash. Sweet-Ade would be a cash fiend because it was borrowing and bringing in new equity partners. This also dilutes Sweet-Ade's ownership from 100 percent to 75 percent, and owning less of a business is almost never a good thing. Cash fiends have posted an annual gain of 5.75 percent, which is 4.25 percent lower per year than the market; if the same weak performance persists, the cash fiends would lose relative to the market by almost 1,200 percent over a 30-year period.[8]

Of course, not every company that falls into one of these first three groups loses relative to the market. Rapid expansion, overzealous acquisitions, and tons of cash raising can lead to big short-term gains in earnings—and therefore great paydays for CEOs—but these corporate strategies have foretold weak performance for stock investors. It doesn't help that the average tenure of CEOs is shortening: during the second half of the twentieth century, CEOs often held their posts for 10 to 15 years, but in the first decade of the twenty-first century, the average tenure for CEOs at the world's largest 2,500 publicly traded firms fell from 8.1 years to 6.3 years.[9] Shorter tenures will likely lead to shorter-term thinking, which may continue to spell trouble for equity investors in the future. We can't fault CEOs for being self-interested, but we need to focus on what is best for us as investors. And that brings us to the final group of companies, the stakeholder stewards.

Stakeholder Stewards.   This final group is the direct opposite of the cash fiends. These companies are paying down debt and sending cash back *to* shareholders in the form of dividends or share repurchases. They are operating efficient businesses because they generate enough cash to reduce their debts and reward shareholders. As we saw with the Sector Stewards strategy in the last chapter, companies that reward shareholders have performed extremely well across market history. But the sector strategy was just a concentrated list of ten stocks. Stakeholder stewards are the 10 percent of companies that have returned the most cash to stakeholders in the past twelve months. They have posted an annual gain of 15.4 percent, which is 5.4 percent per year *higher* than the S&P 500. If the same outstanding performance persists, the Stewards would beat the market by more than 5,700 percent over a 30-year period.[10]

Of course, every CEO should make all of his or her decisions based on what is in the best interest of their shareholders. But CEOs (and other key executives) are only human, and often their decisions destroy, rather than create, shareholder value because they misallocate their cash or because they are too reliant on outsiders to raise cash. The best companies to own are ones whose managers are using a sizable chunk of their cash to pay regular dividends to their shareholders, repurchase shares from their shareholders, and pay down debt owed to creditors.

Rule #1 for the Millennial Money strategy is to buy companies that are returning cash to shareholders and/or paying down debt. There is a very simple way to identify these kinds of companies. Look for companies with large negative "financing" cash flows relative to their overall market value. Negative financing cash flows result when companies pay dividends, repurchase shares, or pay down debt (they are negative because cash is leaving the company). Positive financing cash flows result when companies borrow from creditors or sell new equity shares to the market. Overall market value is just the size of the company. We will call this ratio of financing cash flows to market value "stakeholder yield."

Buying High-Quality Businesses

When Warren Buffet first started investing, he followed the lessons he learned from Ben Graham to find companies trading at a discount to the value of their net assets. He would often compare this strategy to finding cigarette butts and taking one last puff. These companies were often very *bad* companies—and priced accordingly—but the market was too harsh on them and had left them underpriced. Buffett could take the market equivalent of one last puff from these downtrodden companies and make a tidy profit. As his investing philosophy evolved over the years, he has moved from buying bad companies at extremely low prices to buying good companies at fair prices. He ultimately made his fortune in enduring, high-quality companies like American Express and

Coca-Cola—far cries from the cigarette butts of his early investing career. There are two rules (rules #2 and #3) that we will use
to identify great companies for the Millennial Money strategy.
These two attributes are the rate of return that a company earns on
its investments (rule #2) and the quality of a company's earnings
(rule #3). Summed up, we want to invest in profitable companies whose earnings come from real cash flows rather than from
accounting gimmicks. Let's look at both rules.

Rule #2—Return on Investment

When we buy a stock, we do so because we want the highest possible return on our investment—if we lose money on our investments, we get pissed off. If we invest $10,000 in the stock market
and a year later have $12,000, then we've earned $2,000, which is
a 20 percent return on our investment. We want the highest return
possible, and companies do too. Instead of buying stocks, companies make investments in property, equipment, people, projects,
and so on. Just as we can evaluate the returns of our portfolios, we
can evaluate the returns earned by companies using a measurement called "return on invested capital." We calculate it exactly
the same way that we calculate returns for our own portfolios:
Earnings (like the $2,000 earned above) divided by total amount
invested ($10,000 above).[11]

It may seem obvious that we should buy companies that are
making money, but since 1990, an average of 20 percent of companies have lost money in any given annual period. We want to buy
companies that are earning positive returns because businesses
that have earned great returns on their investments are themselves
great investments. Companies in the top 10 percent by return on
invested capital have grown by 13 percent per year since 1965,
significantly higher than the market's 9.6 percent annual return

during the same period. That compounds to a 2,350 percent advantage over 30-year periods. Companies that are the best "investors" have positive earnings and are obviously smart with their investment choices because they've earned so much on them.

Rule #2 is to buy companies that earn high returns on their investments.

Rule #3—Quality Profits

To many investors, the most important number that any company reports to its shareholders is earnings—the proverbial bottom line. Earnings are the *so what* of any report released by global public companies, and it is the number that matters most to investors. On financial news networks, programming will often be interrupted for a breaking "earnings report." Did the company beat expectations? When it does, the stock price will often skyrocket, and when it doesn't, the stock price often nose dives. But investors of all levels pay too much attention to bottom-line earnings; they should instead be focusing on *real cash flows*.

A simple example will illustrate the difference between earnings and cash flows. Let's return to our lemonade stands, Squeezers and Sweet-Ade, which both "earn" $100 on one Sunday afternoon. Squeezers sells 100 cups for $1 each and is paid entirely in cash. Sweet-Ade sells the same 100 cups, but one large customer buys 20 cups and doesn't have the cash to pay, so he takes the lemonade and promises to pay the next day. If these were corporations, then both would report that they had earnings of $100 on Sunday, but Squeezers also would have reported $100 of cash flow, whereas Sweet-Ade would only have had $80 of cash flow. The remaining $20 would be entered into "accounts receivable," or money owed by customers for services already rendered. In a similar scenario, let's say Squeezers bought one box of lemonade mix for $10 and used it all to make lemonade, which was sold one sunny Sunday for $100. That would mean $100 of sales, $10 of cost, and $90 of earnings (and, in this case, $90 of cash flow). Sweet-Ade bought three boxes for $30, but only one box-worth of lemonade sells on Sunday. By traditional reporting standards, Sweet-Ade would have $100 of sales, $10 of cost (the cost of what was sold), and therefore $90 in earnings just like Squeezers. But Sweet-Ade's cash flow would have been just $70 because of the overinvestment in lemonade mix (i.e, inventory).

These are just two of the ways that earnings can look higher than they really are. Instead of earnings, millennial investors should shift their focus to cash flow. As Alfred Rappaport, one of my favorite writers on earnings and shareholder value, says, "cash is a fact, profit is an opinion."[12] Whose opinion? The corporate managers and financial executives who have the discretion to move spending and profits around to meet short-term Wall Street expectations. The best businesses are ones that generate tons of positive cash flows through their operations, and the worst are those that "create" earnings to satisfy short-term Wall Street expectations at the expense of the long-term health of the company. Cash flow is much harder to fake than earnings and is therefore a much more reliable indicator of success.

"Earnings management" isn't a rare problem. One research group conducted a survey of 401 financial executives and found that firms are often willing to sacrifice shareholder value in order to meet quarterly expectations. Of those surveyed, 78 percent admitted that they would give up shareholder value to smooth earnings reports, and 55 percent said they would avoid projects that would cause them to miss earnings expectations, even if those projects were likely to create large positive value for shareholders down the road.[13] In the survey, 77 percent of financial executives said that meeting expectations helped the "external reputation of management"—meaning they were likely to keep their jobs. As one respondent said, "I miss the target; I'm out of a job." To achieve these comically short-term targets, 80 percent said they would avoid spending on research and development, advertising, and maintenance—all good for the long-term health of the company, but bad for the short-term earnings report.[14] This sort of manipulation is so common because earnings matter to investors and to executives more than they should. In the survey, when asked what number matters the most, 159 executives voted for earnings. Executives voted sales and cash flows for a distant second place, tied with 36 votes each.

We must look a level deeper than earning to cash flow. Because cash flow is so much harder to fake, it is a much better way of evaluating a company's profitability. There is a simple way to find companies with real, not manipulated earnings: take reported earnings, subtract operating cash flows, and divide the result by market capitalization. The resulting number is a measure of the company's earnings quality. The lower the number, the better, because that means that cash flow exceeds earnings—which it should. In the lemonade stand example, cash flow for Sweet-Ade was *less* than earnings—a major red flag. The Millennial Money strategy favors companies with outstanding earnings quality, because quality earnings have historically led to quality returns. The quality leaders (top 10 percent) have grown at an annual rate of 14.4 percent, beating the market by an average of 3,850 percent over 30-year periods.

Rule #3 is to insist on strong cash flows: real earnings, not manipulated earnings.

As Figure 6.1 shows, these first three rules create large excess return over time. Since 1972, a $1 investment in the market has

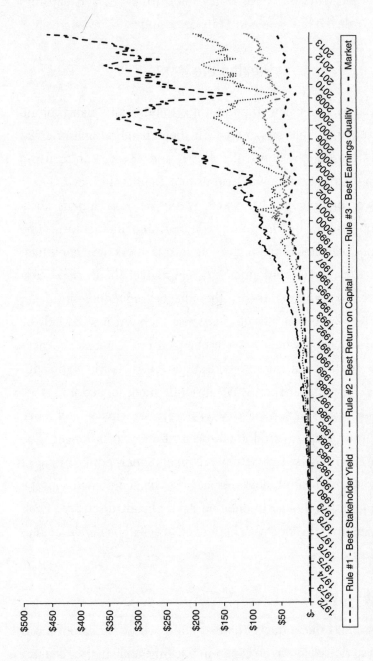

Figure 6.1   Rules #1, #2, and #3. Growth of $1

- - - Rule #1 - Best Stakeholder Yield · - · - Rule #2 - Best Return on Capital ········· Rule #3 - Best Earnings Quality - · - · Market

grown to $57. But a $1 investment in stocks with the best stakeholder yield (rule #1), return on capital (rule #2), and earnings quality (rule #3) has grown to $456, $113, and $202, respectively.

Picking the Best

Now that we know how important it is to buy high-quality, profitable companies that are smart with their spending and oriented toward their shareholders (rules #1, #2, and #3), we can focus on two final attributes that will help us pick the best in breed. These final two components of the strategy are the most famous stock-selection criteria in the world: valuation and momentum. The fact that cheap stocks and high-momentum stocks have continued to beat the market confounds efficient-market theorists because according to traditional theory, these factors *should not provide an edge*. The reason that they do is because each is driven entirely by investor behavior, which has not changed one wink since stocks were traded in Exchange Alley, London, in the early eighteenth century. New information is *not* instantly incorporated into stock prices—investors often leave stocks way too cheap, and once momentum starts to build it can persist for a year or longer. The combination of these two attributes is an extremely powerful way of picking market-beating stocks, especially when combined with the quality and shareholder orientation rules already discussed. Each factor has a rich history, with books and articles aplenty devoted to their effectiveness.

Rule #4—Value

In Botswana I met a tracker named Super whose background was very mysterious. He was an expert in tracking game in the Kalahari Desert, where in the very dry winter—when food is scarce—game is very hard to come by. He was so good because he was patient and experienced, and had remarkable eyesight—"like a meerkat." Even though he was elusive, my brother-in-law and I kept trying to pry into his history, because we figured that only a very interesting path could have led him to his current job and skill set. Then one night, the topic of American football came up and he mentioned how badly he wanted a football to toss around. He was well over six feet tall, strong, and had very long arms, so we asked him how far he could throw a ball. He replied "if we all had a throwing contest, I would win." We were a little dubious because my brother-in-law played football in college and had a pretty damn good arm, so we challenged him. Thank God we did because after throwing a rock farther than we could see, he told us about his training where he learned "the hard way" how to survive and track in the bush. He told us that he knew the key spot to attack on every animal to kill it instantly. The hippo, for example, has a soft spot on the roof of its mouth that is only accessible to a spear when the hippo is charging you, mouth open, and is seconds from mauling you to death. He had similar stories for how he'd killed charging buffalo, ostrich, and antelope. In our eyes, Super jumped from an interesting guide to a legend—he had faced intense fear and emerged stronger.

I am sure that anyone would share our awe at Super's stories—even if they were embellished or untrue—because we love the idea of facing our fears rather than running from them. The same holds true in the investing world, where the great legends have succeeded because they have faced market fear, buying when all others were terrified by the market. John Templeton was fond of buying at "points of maximum pessimism" because the prices associated with pessimism were so attractive. Saying you will buy low is one thing, but actually *buying* in the face of wildly negative market sentiment is another thing altogether. It is the market equivalent of standing one's ground against a charging hippo. Templeton was also famous for buying out-of-favor companies as the world plunged into World War II in 1939. He bought 100 shares of every company (all 104 of them) trading below a dollar. His purchases in a time of fear netted him a fortune.[15]

Value investing is all about buying in the face of fear, pessimism, and negativity, and it is *value* that is the most crucial piece of the Millennial Money strategy. The attributes I've discussed to this point are important, but it doesn't matter how great a company is if it is overpriced. Even companies with impressive, high-quality earnings and a commitment to shareholders can become bad investments when their stock price gets too high. There is a perfect example of this happening as I write. In 2013, investors around the world were searching anywhere they could for investments that would yield income, because bonds—the dominant income option—were offering pathetically low yields. Baby boomers continue to retire in large numbers, so income-producing investments are important to them. As a result of the clamor for yield, US dividend-paying stocks—which are usually cheap compared to their non-dividend-paying brethren—were bid up by the market until they became one of the most expensive areas of the stock market. Historically, companies with the highest dividend yields are cheaper than other stocks 94 percent of the time (based on the price/earnings ratio). Usually, the average US high-yielding stock trades at a 25 percent discount to other stocks: since 1962, the average price for large US stocks has been 17.4 times their collective earnings, while the average price for high yielding stocks has been 12.6 times their collective earnings.[16] But in 2013, as investors piled into US dividend payers in a mad dash for income, the discount vanished. As of

September 2013, this group of high yielders, including names like Johnson & Johnson and McDonald's, traded at a 13 percent *premium* to the average stock, as opposed to its usual discount. This is a perfect example of good companies that the market got too excited about, in this case because they pay nice dividends. An emphasis on valuation will help you avoid traps like this in the future.

Valuation should be an anchor for *every* investment strategy. The most consistent lesson that we've learned from stock market history is that the less you pay for an investment, the more you are likely to earn from it. Sadly, this is *much* easier said than done. As we saw with the Sector Bargains strategy in chapter 5, the stocks that are cheap at any given market moment tend to be associated with gloom and doom rather than with eagerness and excitement. As exemplified by Templeton's wartime purchases, or by Buffett's early value-investing career, value investing is contrary investing. The cheapest stocks are the ones the market has the lowest expectations for in the future. When other investors are fearful or have extremely low expectations for a company, they often underprice it, but the price eventually rebounds when the market realizes that investors were overly pessimistic.

The reason it's so difficult to be a contrarian value investor is that cheap prices result from trouble. Trouble can come in the form of bad earnings, management incompetence, loss of competitive edge, or negative rumors. Buying as others are bailing out is hard to do because humans hate the prospect of being alone and wrong. But history shows that in the stock market, trouble is opportunity's best disguise. Trouble for any stock—and the resulting price—is a perception. Our money will be made when perception (price) is different from reality (fundamentals like cash flow). This may all sound like value investing is akin to sprinting toward disaster, but really it's more about running toward *perceived* disaster. Clearly, some stocks are cheap for good reason, which is why all the other attributes I've covered in this chapter are a part of the strategy; being contrary works best when you also have additional evidence that the market has got it wrong and the stock is a good investment.

There are many ways to measure valuation, and the best approach is one that combines attributes like price-to-sales, price-to-earnings, and price-to-cash flow ratios, but for the reason explored above, I believe that if you are to choose a single metric, cash flow is the best. There are two kinds of cash flow that you can use, both of which work very well. The first is price-to-operating cash flow, which is just price divided by the cash generated from the normal business activities of a company. The second, and more refined, version is to compare a company's total "enterprise" value to its *free* cash flow.[17] Free cash flow is operating cash flow minus any spending on property, equipment, land, and other investments. This free cash flow is what is left over even after the company makes the required investments to maintain and grow the business. Where possible, free cash flow is a superior measure to use because it accounts for the empire-builder effect discussed earlier. Still, both options work very well. The cheapest stocks by price-to-cash flow and enterprise-value-to-free cash flow have grown at an annual rate of 16.1 percent and 15.9 percent, respectively, both beating the market's 10 percent return in the same period.

Value will continue to work, because there will always be stocks that are too out of favor and others that are selling at too dear a price. By avoiding the expensive stocks and buying the cheap ones, you will achieve market-beating returns.

Rule #4 is never pay too much for any stock, no matter how fantastic the company. In the stock market, the less you pay, the more you will earn.

Rule #5—Momentum

Value will always matter but sometimes value investments take a long time to turn in the investor's favor and—let's face it—we millennials don't like waiting too long for anything. Luckily, we can use momentum to help us determine *when* to buy cheap stocks. Focusing on value is the best way to identify stocks that are out of favor and where perception may be far worse than reality. The problem with some value stocks is that they are cheap for good reason, and the market won't start loving them again anytime soon. Momentum helps avoid this problem because, as Willie Nelson said, "The early bird gets the worm, but the second mouse gets the cheese." I don't know about you, but I'll take the cheese any day. If we can identify cheap stocks that the market is *just beginning to notice*, we can make our strategy even more effective, and avoid having to wait years for the market to recognize the real value of the cheap stocks in our portfolio.

As the Sector Winners strategy from chapter 5 revealed, high-momentum stocks have delivered outstanding returns to investors for decades. Simply buying stocks that have gone up the most in the past six months has been an easy—but admittedly very risky—way of beating the market. The high-momentum strategy has produced a return of 15.2 percent annually and easily trounced the market's 10 percent return in the same period, but momentum stocks are 50 *percent* more volatile than the market, so to be a pure momentum investor you'd have to have a very high tolerance for periods of weak performance.[18] There have been numerous occasions when the high-momentum portfolio loses relative to the market by more than 15 percent in a one-year period, and one occasion when it lagged the market by 35 percent! Can you imagine sticking with a strategy following a year

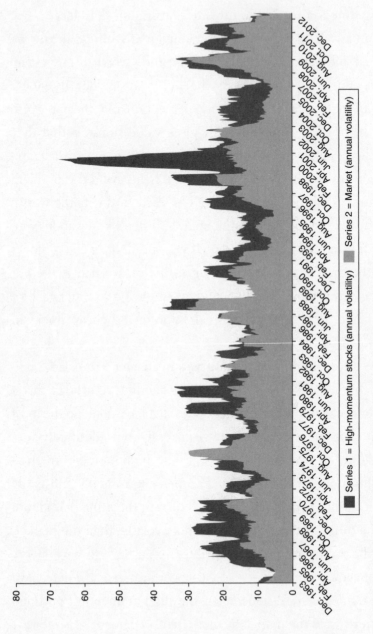

Figure 6.2   High-Momentum Stocks Much More Volatile than the Market

Series 1 = High-momentum stocks (annual volatility)   Series 2 = Market (annual volatility)

when you trailed the market by that much? Me neither. Figure 6.2 shows that high-momentum stocks are much more volatile than the overall market.

Momentum works much better when we combine it with value, which is how we will use it in the Millennial Money strategy. Here's why: if every year all we did was buy the cheapest stocks in the world (the cheapest 20 percent) we'd have a nice strategy that has, historically, grown at an annual rate of 15.3 percent, turning $10,000 into $716,000 in an average 30-year period. But within that universe of cheap stocks, we can be the second mouse who gets the cheese by focusing on cheap stocks that have the strongest recent momentum. If we buy stocks that are in the cheapest 20 percent but then also in the fastest growing 20 percent, the result jumps up to an annual rate of 17.2 percent, turning $10,000 into $1,180,000. The flipside would be stocks that are cheap but still doing poorly in the market over the last six months (the bottom 20 percent by six-month momentum), and they have a much less impressive return of 11.7 percent, turning $10,000 into $277,000. That means that even if we are smart investors who insist on cheap valuations, momentum can mean a difference of nearly $1,000,000 over a 30-year investment horizon.

Since the 1920s, momentum investing has led to great results. Cheap stocks can stay cheap for a long time, so for the Millennial Money strategy we focus only on stocks that have just begun their comeback.

Rule #5 is find stocks that the market is just starting to notice.

Bringing It All Together

Now that we have all these powerful rules for picking stocks, it is time to combine them into one strategy. Finding stocks that screen well by all these criteria is rare, so we want to find the best combination of attributes that we can. The beautiful thing about the Millennial Money strategy is that no further work is required once these rules are applied. For the companies that meet each rule, we don't need to know anything about the CEO, the length of his tenure, or her plans for the future. While there may be some edge to be gained by knowing details like these, it is impossible to know these details for each of the thousands of companies trading around the globe. A simple checklist will get us most of the way there, with minimal effort.

There are two ways to bring all the ideas in this chapter together: a checklist approach—in the spirit of Atul Gawande—and a ranking approach. I will describe both, because depending on which tool you use to screen for these stocks, one or the other may be more convenient. Both are fantastic ways to find the best current stocks for investment. If you do not want to do the screening yourself, there are many other options that make use of this general style of investing, where several attributes are combined into one strategy. As smart indexes become more and more sophisticated, they will likely use multiple factors like those I have discussed. Perhaps the most famous is Joel Greenblatt's Magic Formula, which looks for stocks with both great valuations and great profitability—a two-factor model that is an improvement on the myriad one-factor options currently available. Here is a quick review of the attributes that we are looking for:

Stakeholder Yield.   The best companies will be those that are buying back shares, paying dividends, and paying down debt. The worst will be borrowing like crazy and issuing new equity shares to raise more cash, diluting existing shareholders in the process. Shareholder yield is calculated as financing cash flow relative to market value.

Return on Invested Capital.   We want to invest with companies that are themselves good investors. The higher the return any company earns on its own investments, the better. Return on invested capital is calculated as operating earnings divided by invested capital.

Earnings Quality.   The easiest measurement of earnings quality is to subtract cash flow from earnings and divide the result by the company's market capitalization. The lower the number, the better, because a low number means that cash flows are greater than earnings. The low number will steer us toward companies with the strongest cash flows relative to their earnings. Note that we cannot just subtract cash flow from earnings (without also scaling by market value), because that would not account for the relative size of the company—we must divide by market capitalization.

Price to Cash Flow or Enterprise Value to Free Cash Flow.   As we've seen, cash flows are often ignored in favor of earnings, but they are a much cleaner measure of success. Companies trading with very low price to cash flow are companies for which the market has very low expectations. This is a great way of identifying situations where perception is much more negative than reality.

Six-Month Momentum.   This is a stock's total return over the past six months. Total return includes any dividends paid by the company during the six-month period and any change in price. So, for example, if Google's stock price was $1,000 six months ago and has risen to $1,200 today, then Google's stock return was 20 percent over the past six months assuming it didn't pay any dividends. If it had paid dividends, then its return would have been even higher. Buying stocks with strong recent returns has worked extremely well—it helps us find stocks that the market is starting to notice.

*   *   *

It is important to note that while I've developed an argument for and against certain factors (e.g., using cash flow instead of earnings), the general themes are more important than the specific factors. Price/earnings is still a great way to find cheap stocks, I just prefer the more intuitive approach of using cash flows because they are harder for managers to manipulate. Variants of all of these ideas will likely work in the future, so experimentation is encouraged!

The Checklist

First up is the Millennial Money checklist. One rule for each of the factors that we have discussed:

- ☑ Stakeholder yield is greater than 5 percent
- ☑ Return on invested capital is greater than 30 percent
- ☑ Operating cash flow is greater than reported profits (earnings quality)
- ☑ Enterprise-value-to-free cash flow is less than 10 times
- ☑ Six-month momentum in the top three-quarters of the market

Since 1973, this checklist results in an average of 26 stocks at any given time—a very concentrated portfolio. Like the checklist for the central-line-insertion procedure, none of these items is revolutionary, but in combination they work remarkably well.

The growth rate for this Millennial Money checklist blows the doors off of all other strategies we have explored to this point.

Since 1973, companies passing this checklist have grown at an annual rate of 19.95 percent, almost double the growth rate for the market during the same period. That means that in an average 30-year period, a $10,000 investment would surge to $2.35 million. *That is more than twelve times the amount that you would earn if you had invested in the overall market*, which earned 10 percent per year.

As we near the end of the second part of our investing formula—being different—it is important to highlight just how unique the portfolios are that result from using this checklist. Recalling the concept of "active share" from the last chapter, where the percentage active share indicates what percent of the portfolio is different from the market; this strategy has an active share of more than 90 percent and often reaches 95 percent. Sometimes more than half of the portfolio is invested in consumer stocks; other times less than 10 percent is invested in consumer stocks. The stocks, industries, and sectors that look most attractive vary over time.

But the DNA of the portfolio—the attributes upon which our rules and strategy are built—remain constant. These attributes are like our red X's on Seinfeld's calendar—so long as we stick with them, they will help us beat the market. On average, these stocks have a stakeholder yield of 10 percent—so for every $100 of market cap, they are returning $10 to stakeholders. They trade for an average of less than five times cash flow—twice as cheap as normal stock, which trades for eleven times cash flow. Not only are they cheap and smart with their cash, but they earn 40 percent returns on their investments (return on investment capital) and have recent market returns in the top third of the market—they are just being noticed.

The first step toward building a fortune is making a commitment to consistent contributions to your investment account, hopefully at least 10 percent of your income. With this checklist, we can then earn returns significantly higher than the market.

The Ranking Approach

The second approach does not set minimum thresholds for each of our attributes but instead searches for stocks with the best combination of them all. For the sake of simplicity, if there are 100 stocks in the world, each one is ranked 1 to 100 on each of our five key attributes, and those five scores are averaged for an overall score 1 to 100. We then buy the top ranking 10 to 50 stocks (depending on how concentrated you want your portfolio to be). This approach provides more flexibility than the checklist approach, because you can create portfolios of any size that you want. Sometimes the checklist approach produces very few stocks, so the ranking approach is a nice substitute to guarantee a certain number of stocks in your portfolio. The results are very similar: the annual growth rate for the Millennial Money strategy using a 25-stock version of the ranking approach is 20.2 percent, just slightly higher than the checklist approach.

Using the Millennial Money Strategy

There are several free and several premium stock screeners that can help you run the Millennial Money strategy for yourself. The easiest option is to join the American Association of Individual Investors (AAII)—a fantastic resource for investors in general— which will list the stocks that are currently passing the Millennial Money checklist. You can access it on AAII's website at www.aaii. com, which charges a very reasonable annual fee. Their website also tracks other similar stock-selection strategies so you can browse and find one that best suits you.

Another great option is www.portfolio123.com. It offers sophisticated but easy-to-use screening tools. Other screening options are Yahoo Finance (free, http://screener.finance.yahoo.com /newscreener.html), FinViz (free, http://finviz.com), and the bloodhound system (premium, for larger accounts, http://www. bloodhoundsystem.com). Not all screeners will allow you to replicate the strategy exactly, but most will have similar factors for you to work with. For example, you may need to specify that the price-to-earnings ratio be less than 15 rather than using free cash flow.

In your brokerage account, you'd then buy an equal amount of each stock passing the checklist. If there are 20 stocks, you'd invest 5 percent of your portfolio in each. You can then refresh (rebalance) the portfolio just once a year. Trading just once a year saves time and it is tax friendly. You can hold any stocks that are at a gain until they become long-term capital gains, which will be taxed at a lower rate. This is the simplest way to implement the strategy, but in chapter 10 I will further explain how to spread your trading out over the entire year to achieve smoother results.

Cost Matters

These results speak for themselves, but they do not come free. You'll either pay trading costs (if you do it yourself) or management fees (if you hire someone who runs a similar strategy). As noted in chapter 5, one of the two main advantages of index funds and index ETFs is that they charge extremely low fees—and low fees mean better investor returns over the long term. Professionally managed strategies that use the factors I have discussed will be more expensive than index funds because they offer a premium

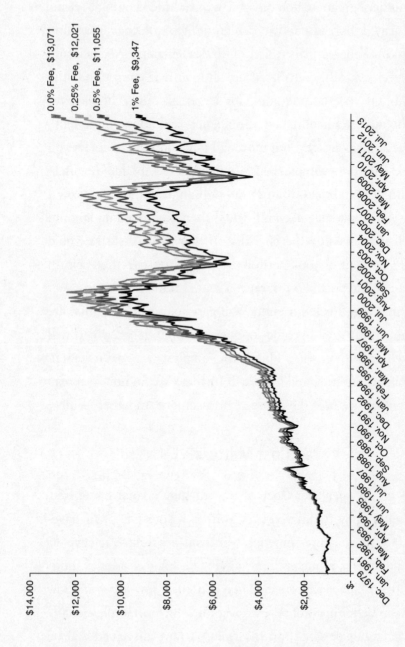

Figure 6.3   Growth of $1,000 Invested in S&P 500 Index Fund at Four Different Fee Levels. Fee levels: 0.0%, 0.25%, 0.5%, and 1%

service. As proponents of index funds are quick to point out, the *average* manager does not earn their fees because they lose to the market once fees and trading costs are taken out of total returns. John Bogle calls this problem the "tyranny of compounding costs," and for good reason. If two managers had identical portfolios that delivered 10 percent returns before fees, but one charged 1 percent fees instead of 0.5 percent, the additional costs would balloon from just 0.5 percent in any one year to 195 percent over 30 years— tyranny indeed. Examples like this are why Bogle is also fond of saying, "you get what you *don't* pay for."[19] Figure 6.3 shows the growth of $1,000 invested in the S&P 500 30 years ago, in 1980. Depending on the fee charged, the ending values can be very different. An S&P 500 index fund with no fee would have turned $1,000 into $13,071. But if the index fund charged 1 percent, the ending value would have been considerably lower: $9,347.

We millennials should be extremely conscious of the fees we pay, because compounding magnifies their importance over time. But we should balance our desire for low fees with our desire for excess returns. After all, if a smart index or custom portfolio strategy earns 2 to 10 percent more than the market per year, higher fees are certainly justified. Let's assume that for the checklist version of the strategy we are charged a 1.5 percent fee and that trading costs are an additional 0.25 percent. Both are at the high end of what a strategy like this would cost to implement. With those costs removed, the return drops from 19.95 percent to 18.2 percent. Instead of finishing the average 30-year period with $2.3 million, we'd end with $1.5 million. That is a big drop, but it is still more than eight times what we would earn in a market index fund. The tyranny of compounding costs should be avoided whenever possible, but paying more for a far superior strategy also makes sense.

The Millennial Money Strategy for the Future

My confidence in this strategy is supreme because the attributes that it searches for make intuitive sense, have worked exceptionally well across market history, and take advantage of common behavioral mistakes that will continue into the future. The market funnels the collective psychology of its participants into stock prices. This includes emotions, aversions, and desires. It is natural to want to buy stocks that are doing very well and that the market loves. But this is a path to failure because expensive stocks have terrible returns. Investors will continue to overemphasize the importance of earnings reports, chase the most popular stocks, and neglect how corporate managers spend their hard-earned cash. Luckily these common mistakes create opportunities that can lead to incredible long-term portfolio returns, and therefore to impressive fortunes.

Seinfeld's career blossomed in part because he always persevered. Peter Pronovost's checklist (his strategy) saved lives because it forced doctors to be more consistent. Now that you have the right strategy for selecting stocks, you need a similar strategy for making sure you stick with it through anything the market might throw at you. This brings us to the crucial final section of the book: how to get out of your own way.

7

———

GET OUT OF YOUR OWN WAY

While going global and being different is a great plan, we must avoid the problem best summed up by Iron Mike Tyson, who said "Everybody has a plan until they get punched in the face." It's one thing to agree with a plan or strategy, it's another thing to execute it. The stock market has many ways of punching us in the face, whether it is a rapid panic and crash or a long period of underperformance. It is enduring these tough times that make any strategy work. Because you are only human, there is a good chance that you will get in your own way at some point; that is unless you take steps ahead of time to keep your emotions in check. This chapter explains why we aren't wired to be good investors, the negative impact our wiring has had on investor returns, and why the best way to avoid making big mistakes is to make investing automatic.

Twins and the Investor's Brain

Oskar Stohr and Jack Yufe met for the first time in Minnesota in 1979; they were both 46 years old. Oskar was raised as a Roman

Catholic in Czechoslovakia and once planned to join the Hitler Youth; Jack was raised by a Jewish father in Trinidad. Despite their wildly different upbringings, Oskar and Jack had a lot in common. They were both outgoing and impatient, read books from back to front, flushed the toilet before *and* after use, dipped buttered toast in their coffees, and liked to fake a sneeze during awkward silences.[1] It is sad that they did not meet until age 46, because Oskar and Jack were identical twins that had been reared apart. They were one pair of many similar identical twins who were reunited for the famous Minnesota twins study at the University of Minnesota in 1979.[2] Like Oskar and Jack, other pairs of reared-apart twins shared remarkably strange behaviors despite different environmental influences. When another pair—Barbara and Daphne—met for the first time, they were both wearing beige dresses and brown velvet jackets. They quickly learned that they both took their coffee black and cold and that they both had an odd habit of pushing up their nose—and both called the habit "squidging."[3] A third pair, Jim and Jim, each had first wives named Linda and second wives named Betty and each had a son named James Allen (although one spelled it Alan). Both drove light blue Chevys and worked as part-time sheriffs.[4] These amazing stories, along with more formal evaluations of IQ and personality (the Minnesota Multiphasic Personality Inventory), revealed just how dominant our genes are in determining our behavioral tendencies. As Nancy Segal, one of the researchers in the Minnesota twins study, said in her book on the subject, "If pressed to produce a bottom line, it must be that reared apart twins show that genetic influence is pervasive, affecting virtually every measured behavioral trait, many previously assumed to be environmental in origin."[5] A lot of our behavior is coded into our brains, and there is no escaping our programming.

Identical-twin behavior also provides useful insight into the "investor's brain." To test how influential genes are on our investing choices, a group of researchers studied the investment decisions made by identical and fraternal twins from Sweden. The Swedish government keeps impressive data on identical and fraternal twins—and also records the investing activity of Swedish citizens—so the Swedish twins made for perfect subjects. Identical twins share 100 percent of their genes but fraternal twins share just 50 percent on average, so if certain behaviors are more common between identical twins than they are between fraternal twins, it indicates that there is a genetic component to those behaviors. In their fascinating paper entitled "Why Do Individuals Exhibit Investment Biases?," researchers Henrik Cronqvist and Stephan Siegel found that just as odd behaviors in pairs of "Minnesota" twins were genetic in nature, many common investor mistakes are also written in our genes.

The study found that several of the most common investor mistakes—including the bias toward stocks in one's home country, the tendency to chase performance and trade too often, and the reluctance to sell losing stocks—are highly genetic. For each behavior tested, identical twins were more likely to share damaging investing biases than fraternal twins. As the authors of the study concluded,

> a long list of investment biases…are "human," in the sense that we are born with them. We base this conclusion on empirical evidence that genetic factors explain up to 50% of the variation in these biases across individuals. The psychological mechanisms behind the investment biases have apparently survived natural selection over hundreds of thousands of years, presumably because they maximize (or in a hunter-gatherer society, used to maximize) the likelihood of human survival and reproduction.[6]

These findings typify the modern investor's plight. We are pro-grammed to maximize our chances for survival, but the instincts that kept us alive in the savannah get us killed in the stock market.

It is amazing that twins are more likely to share investing behaviors, but the most important finding of the twins investor study was that we are born with the tendency to make investing mistakes—they are prewired into our brains. While the study showed that the *magnitude* of our various investment biases are genetic, all investors have a purely "human" problem: as a species, we just aren't cut out to make smart investing choices. Psychologist Philip Zimbardo expresses our problem this way:

> Because of the rapid change in the world around us since our birth, we humans are living anachronisms. Our world has changed dramatically in the past 150 years. Human physiology, in contrast, took millions of years to create and has not changed much in 150,000 years. Your body—even if it is in mint condition—is designed for success in the past. It is an antique biological machine that evolved in response to a world that no longer exists. Although we live in a world in which computer processing speed doubles roughly every twenty-four months, human information processing has not expanded substantially over the past 150,000 years. Our physiology is clearly behind the times.[7]

Stock markets as we think of them are only a few hundred years old, and we are ill equipped to handle them.

The "Human" Tax

Thanks to the way human beings are wired, the average investor earns returns considerably lower than the market. The easiest way to measure our "human" problem is to compare two different kinds of returns: a buy-and-hold return and a behavior-adjusted return. To understand the difference, consider the following hypothetical example. If you had invested $10,000 in the S&P 500 in July 1993, and simply held on for twenty years, your investment would have grown at an annual rate of 8.7 percent and turned your initial $10,000 into $52,600.[8] We will call this first type of return a buy-and-hold return, but very few investors just buy and hold. Instead, they invest additional cash when the market looks appealing and sell some of their investments when things look scary. Many investors, for example, started investing tons of money in 1999 as the technology bubble inflated, and sold a large part of their portfolio in early 2009 near the bottom of the market crash; they bought high and sold low. So let's say a second investor made the same initial $10,000 investment in 1993, but then added $15,000 in January 2000 because of the market excitement, and sold $15,000 in February 2009 because he was scared that the market might continue to tumble. These mistimed decisions would have reduced his annual return from 8.7 percent to 5.5 percent, and he'd have finished the twenty years with $41,600. This second return is the one that is *actually earned* by investors; we will call it the behavior-adjusted return.

In the real world, almost every example comparing buy-and-hold returns to behavior-adjusted returns shows that the behavior-adjusted returns are significantly worse than the buy-and-hold returns. The oldest saying in the stock market is "buy low and sell high," but instead investors buy at market peaks, excited by all the money being made in the market, and sell at market bottoms, terrified that they might lose everything. Their programming makes them chase strong recent trends and run from scary trends when they should be doing the opposite.

My hypothetical example may seem extreme because I've chosen the two worst times to move into (January 2000) and out of (February 2009) the market, but there are countless similar real-world examples. For the Vanguard S&P 500 index fund—one of the world's largest funds—the buy-and-hold return was 5.01 percent for the 15 years ending in October 2013, but the behavior-adjusted return was 3.49 percent. The behavior-adjusted returns are even worse for "hot" mutual funds. Consider the 200 mutual funds with the highest inflows in the late 1990s—the most popular funds where investors put the most cash. Between 1996 and 2005, the average buy-and-hold return for these popular 200 funds was 8.9 percent. But the real, behavior-adjusted return that investors earned in those same 200 mutual funds was just 2.4 percent.[9] There are even more extreme examples. I looked up the fund that had the best overall returns over the past five years and found the Oceanstone Fund, and over those same five years the buy-and-hold return was 28 *percent per year higher* than the behavior-adjusted return.[10] This happens because investors rush in after the largest returns have already been earned.

We can take an even broader, industry-wide look at mutual fund flows and the same trend holds true. Figure 7.1 shows the amount, in millions of dollars, that investors are either buying or selling at any given time across all stock mutual funds. Inflows peaked in early 2000, near the peak of the Internet bubble, and outflows peaked in early 2009, near the bottom of the latest severe bear market. These two decisions were collectively devastating for stock market investors. After inflows into the stock market peaked in 2000, the MSCI All Country World Index collapsed by nearly 50 percent. Since outflows peaked in February 2009, the All Country World Index is up 125 percent.[11] Investors were on the wrong side of both trades.

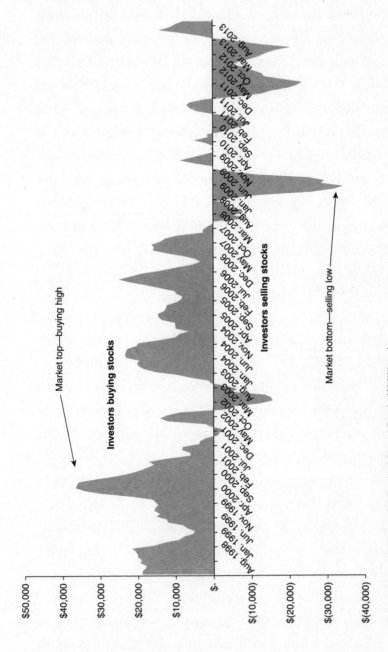

Figure 7.1 Net Flows for Equity Mutual Funds ($Millions)

Source: Fund flows from Investment Company Institute

All these examples illustrate why our behavior acts like a tax on our wealth. A loss of even 1 to 2 percent worth of return per year due to behavioral mistakes can quickly compound into much larger return gaps. Take the example of the Vanguard S&P 500 index fund from above, where investors earned a behavior-adjusted return of 3.49 percent over the past 15 years—1.5 percent per year lower than the buy-and-hold return of 5.01 percent.[12] Over 15 years, $100 invested at the behavior-adjusted return grows to $167, but $100 invested at the buy-and-hold return grows to $208. That's a "human tax" rate of 20 percent. As the holding period gets longer, the human tax rate gets worse. If the same gap persisted for a 30-year holding period, the human tax would jump to 35 percent—a huge chunk of overall returns.

Buy High, Sell Low

The American Association of Individual Investors (AAII), which was founded in 1978, is a nonprofit organization with 150,000 subscribers; its mission is to educate investors and help them achieve their investing goals. Since 1987, it has surveyed its members, asking about their market sentiment and about their current asset allocation between stocks, bonds, and cash.

These sentiment and asset-allocation surveys provide great long-term insight into the investors brain, and the historical data from AAII's surveys are fascinating. Over the long term, the average AAII member had invested 60 percent in stocks, 16 percent in bonds, and 24 percent in cash. But the allocation to stocks has varied from 40 percent to nearly 80 percent as the stock market has waxed and waned over the years. In a classic example of buying high and selling low that mirrors the industry flows in Figure 7.1, the highest allocation to stocks (77 percent) came in

January and March 2000, at the absolute peak of the Internet bubble, and the lowest allocation to stocks (41 percent) came in March 2009, at what turned out to be the exact market bottom after the credit-crisis-led market crash.

Allocations between stocks, bonds, and cash are the result of investor sentiment. When investors are most bullish about the future, they overweight stocks; when they are most bearish, they underweight them. AAII also maintains a survey of this stock-market sentiment, asking members whether they are "bullish," "neutral," or "bearish" about the stock market over the next six months. If we throw out the neutral votes, we can create a "sentiment" score by subtracting the bullish percentage from the bearish percentage. The sentiment score was at its most bullish (optimistic) on January 6, 2000, when 75 percent were bullish but only 13 percent were bearish. Investors were the most bearish (pessimistic) on March 5, 2009, when just 19 percent were bullish and 70 percent were bearish. The market bottom was reached on March 9, 2009. The stock market is extremely hard to time, but this is an example of perfect *mistiming*.

These disappointing behavior-adjusted returns are no secret. Most investing books point to similar evidence that investors underperform the market. So why do these errors persist? Why can't we fix these common mistakes? The main problem is that our behavior is often beyond our control. Our brains process a ridiculous amount of information and most of it is filtered out before consciousness enters the picture. Our brains specialize in the recognition of patterns, threats, and rewards because doing so has helped us survive and procreate. We shun danger and seek rewards, but in the stock market, the perception of immediate danger (e.g., in March 2009) often signals long-term opportunity, and the perception of immediate reward (e.g., in March 2000) often signals long-term danger. There is a wonderful book whose title hints at what we *should* do in the stock market, called *What Makes Your Brain Happy and Why You Should Do the Opposite*. In the book, author David DiSalvo says,

> What I wish to communicate with the metaphor of a happy brain is simply that under various conditions, our brains will tend toward a default position that places greatest value on avoiding loss, lessening risk, and averting harm. Our brains have evolved to do exactly that, and much of the time we can be thankful they did. However, these same protective tendencies (what I am calling the tendencies of a "happy brain") can go too far and become obstacles instead of virtues. Our challenge is to know when to think and act contrary to our brain's native leanings.[13]

In light of the perfectly mistimed decisions revealed by the AAII surveys, the answer is that we should act contrary to our own instincts often. But that is very difficult to do because so much of our processing goes on behind the scenes.

The Subconscious Investor—
We Can't Help Ourselves

Have you ever had the feeling that the voice in your head—your inner monologue—is beyond your control? Happens to me all the time. Consciousness—that thing that we call "me" that we think is making all the decisions—is more of an observer than a commander. Much of the processing and decision making goes on behind the scenes, and we simply see the end result. As neuroscientist Michael Gazzaniga says,

> We all feel we are wonderfully unified, coherent mental machines and that our underlying brain structure must somehow reflect

this overpowering sense we all possess. It doesn't. Again, no central command center keeps all other brain systems hopping to the instructions of a five-star general. The brain has millions of local processors making important decisions. It is a highly specialized system with critical networks distributed throughout the 1,300 grams of tissue. *There is no one boss in the brain. You are certainly not the boss of the brain.* Have you ever succeeded in telling your brain to shut up already and go to sleep? (emphasis added)[14]

If this idea sounds strange to you, try three minutes of meditation. Sit down, close your eyes, and attempt to focus on the point of your nose where your breath travels in and out and focus only on your breath. You'll quickly observe that thoughts appear in your mind like bubbles from champagne, seemingly at random and out of nowhere. Do you feel like you scripted those thoughts? When I first did this exercise, I felt like a dog being enticed by 100 different bones at once, pulled in all different directions against my will. My inner monologue was "OK, focus on your breath, in, out...in, out...in...man I'm hungry...I wish this train was shorter than an hour...wow seven years I've been riding this train, that's two hours a day, which is 500 hours a year, which is 3,500 hours since I started working...geez, that's a third of what Malcolm Gladwell says I need to be an expert at something, talk about a waste...oh shit, my breath!" Yet this is how it always is.

Simple things can make a large subconscious impact. If you show the same man a piece of pink cardboard and then test his strength, he will be considerably weaker than he would be after seeing a piece of blue cardboard. A famous study conducted by Professor Alexander Schauss showed that 99 percent of men were weakened after staring at pink cardboard for one minute, but that the same men maintained their normal strength after staring at deep blue cardboard for one minute. As a result of these findings, it became popular to use the color pink in many different ways for its psychological effects. Prisoners were calmer in pink holding cells, charity workers received higher donations wearing pink, and bus companies reduced vandalism by installing pink seats.[15] Because of its power to sedate aggression and promote charity, pink became a useful tool for driving certain desired behaviors.

There is even evidence that brain activity associated with a decision precedes our conscious awareness of having made a decision by up to seven seconds.[16] We like to think we can make cool, calculated decisions using the most evolved and highly reasonable part of our brain (the prefrontal cortex), but we are still slaves to subconscious processing going on in our reptilian and mammalian brains that we share with lizards and monkeys.

There are many similar subconscious cues in the stock market and, whether we like it or not, they have a huge impact on investor behavior. Unfortunately, these subconscious cues tend to lead to many investment mistakes. When a company first starts trading on a stock exchange, following its initial public offering (IPO), it chooses a ticker to represent its stock. AAPL stands for Apple, GE is for General Electric, RSH is for Radio Shack. Amazingly, companies whose ticker symbols are easy to pronounce, like OPEN for Open Table, or HOG for Harley Davidson, have much stronger returns during their first day of trading (15 percent on average) than do stocks whose ticker symbols are difficult to pronounce (7 percent).[17] Of course the fluency of a ticker symbol has nothing to do with the quality of a company, but it does have an impact on the success of an IPO. What's more, things as irrelevant as the weather may have an influence on markets. Between 1982 and 1997, stocks did considerably better in 26 markets around the world on sunny days than they did on cloudy days. The annual return on sunny days in New York City during that period was

24.8 percent, but only 8.7 percent on cloudy days.[18] Sunshine is a quaint example of an environmental influence on our behavior, but other more significant trends exert influence on our choices as well. The economic and market environment in which we grew up has a significant impact on our willingness to take risk. People who have lived through tough economic times and watched stock markets perform poorly are less likely to invest in the stock market, and those that do invest in the stock market put a smaller percentage of their money into stocks because they are perceived as riskier.[19] Because we millennials have come of age during two of the worst stock market crashes in history and lived through the worst economic crisis since the Great Depression, we may take fewer risks than if we'd come of age in the 1980s and '90s. It can be dangerous to our wealth to let what has happened in our past influence what we do with our investments in the future—but it happens all the time.

One advantage of the Millennial Money strategy is that it emphasizes value stocks, which tend to be unloved or neglected by the market. Here again, our brains point us in the opposite direction. Researchers Brad Barber and Terrance Odean found that individual investors tend to shun value stocks and instead buy stocks that get the most attention. They buy more of a stock when it's been in the news or has had a successful day in the market the day before. Our brains are more comfortable with the familiar, and push us toward popular stocks.[20] While our brains like stocks that are getting all the attention, buying those stocks is bad for our portfolios—the stocks that individuals buy tend to underperform those that they sell. As Barber and Odean concluded in their study, "all that glitters is not gold." And as the Sector Leaders and Sector Bargains strategies demonstrated, what glitters in the stock market is often fool's gold—the true treasure does not appear to have such luster.

In another powerful example, young people—specifically young men like me—tend to be overconfident about our abilities, and overconfidence often leads to too much trading. In a study of over 35,000 investment accounts, Barber and Odean found that men trade 45 percent more than women do, and it costs them 2.65 percent per year in lost returns.[21] Women also lose returns by trading too much, but they earn about 1 percent more per year than men do. Single men are the worst offenders—they trade 67 percent more than single women do, and perform 1.4 percent worse per year than single women.[22] Within the same group of 35,000 accounts, age also had an important impact on our trading behavior. The younger the person, the more they traded on average—and the more they traded, the worse their returns. For every decade that we age, the amount that we trade decreases.[23]

We also buy more of stocks that are in the news and have done well recently—that is unless we are exposed to certain Zen influences. When a group of Wall Street professionals were given a pretend $1,000 to invest in their choice of nine different stocks that they could choose based on their recent price charts, they preferred stocks whose price had risen in the recent past. They chose these recent winners over stocks that had gone up and down but mostly sideways; clearly, they expected recent trends to continue. This preference changed, however, when the researcher switched from wearing a plain white T-shirt to a T-shirt with the yin-yang symbol. Because the yin-yang symbol serves as a reminder that things even out over time, its mere presence on the T-shirt led the investors to spend $160 less on the recent winner stocks than they had when the T-shirt was plain white.[24] What's even more amazing is that the effect was stronger among participants who were better traveled or who were more familiar with the meaning of the yin-yang symbol.

Age, the economic environment in which we grew up, ticker symbols, and even the weather are just a few examples of important influences on our behavior as investors. These hurt our returns, so the best way to overcome these influences is to take our behavior out of the equation.

The Fix—Changing Your Default Setting

Default settings have tremendous power. Think about all the e-mails you've received where the signature isn't "Jane Doe" but "Sent from my iPhone." Imagine how much other companies would have to pay in advertising dollars to have their product name appear in hundreds of millions of e-mails! Apple's genius marketing strategy, which harnesses the power of the default option, does it for free. Or consider a much more serious issue: organ donation. In the United States, there are 20,000 organ-transplant surgeries per year, but there would be many more if there were a more plentiful supply of organs. Lack of supply is a major issue in the United States: in 2006 alone, 3,916 people died waiting for a kidney transplant.[25] We don't have enough organs because we don't have enough organ donors. To become a donor in this country, you simply check a box on your driver's license application that says you are willing to donate your organs, but the default setting is to say no to organ donation. This is also known as an opt-in method. But consider two other, very similar countries: Germany and Austria. Germany is also an opt-in country, and only 12 percent of its citizens are organ donors. In Austria, the default option is to be an organ donor, and you must opt out if you don't want your organs used to save lives. In Austria, the organ donation rate is 99 percent![26] Countries around the world that have organ donation as the default have participation rates near 100 percent, and the problem of organ supply is nonexistent. Default options are incredibly powerful tools.

It is scary to realize that our brains incline us toward bad investing choices, but the good news is that by changing your default investing setting you can prevent yourself from making dumb decisions. The easiest solution is to opt in by setting up automatic contributions from your paycheck (or from your bank account) into your investment account(s). If you make your investing automatic, then the faulty programming that precipitates foolish investing decisions won't get in your way.

Usually this decision starts with a 401(k) or similar plan that allows you to make regular contributions to an investment account. Just like organ donation, the choice to make contributions to your 401(k) can be set up by each company as opt in or opt out, and the choice between the two has a huge impact on employee investing decisions. While opting in is as simple as checking a little box, it still requires you to take action. People are lazy and tend to stick with the default option, so opt-in 401(k) plans have low participation rates. But in plans where the default option is to participate—meaning employees must opt out if they want to stop making contributions—the participation rate is much higher. In the 401(k) plan at one large US corporation, the participation rate under the opt-in method was 37.5 percent, but when the company changed to an opt-out plan and made enrollment automatic, participation jumped nearly 50 percent, to 85.9 percent.[27] The gap was even wider among employees at the bottom end of the pay scale, where participation jumped from 12.5 percent to 79.5 percent. Once enrolled, most employees also just left the default allocation options (between stocks, bonds, and cash) when they should have instead tailored their allocations to their age and risk preferences.[28]

The behavior of the employees at this large company illustrates how powerful a default setting can be for investors. If your default is to do nothing, then chances are you won't invest as much as you need to, but if your default is to invest consistently, without any decision making involved, you'll have a nice little nest egg in no time. I invest for a living, and I wasn't always immune to making the same mistakes many investors make. I noticed that I had been avoiding making investments because I was worried that the market had gone up too much (this was several years ago when the market was 50 percent lower than it is today). I missed out on significant returns because I always came up with some reason not to pull the trigger. Finally I set up an automatic plan and that problem went away forever. The first paycheck after making the change was lower than before, but I got used to it quickly and my investment account started growing quietly in the background.

Automatic contributions will probably start with your 401(k), which you should invest in global stock-market indexes or smart indexes/strategies if they are available. The next step will be to open a separate account at an online broker like Charles Schwab and set up an automatic contribution to that account as well.

Taking Control

Our brains are remarkable, but they fail us in the stock market. The evidence from comparing buy-and-hold returns to behavior-adjusted returns is the most powerful indicator that investors have a built-in problem. Sadly the problem isn't something we can easily fix, because so much of our behavior is the result of behind-the-scenes brain processing.

But young investors have an advantage. Knowing in advance that your brain will trick you into making the wrong decisions, you can remove it from the equation. The flexibility to set up automatic contributions and manage your money so easily online gives you a huge advantage over previous generations. You can achieve your goals without making too many decisions and without much effort.

In many ways, the stock market is a system that takes money from the excited and the fearful and gives it to the patient and the disciplined. You can engineer discipline by making investing automatic, and you can learn the power of patience by reframing how you think about time and risk. While you can improve your behavior with automatic solutions, you will still have to make periodic decisions with your money that are independent of your automatic contributions. When making any investing decision, the two biggest mistakes you are likely to make are (1) focusing on the short term and (2) acting on greed or fear. Chapters 8 and 9 explain how to avoid these two errors.

8

THE LONG GAME

My favorite thing about vacation is being unaware of the time. Waking up, going to sleep, and enjoying the day without regard to a schedule is both calming and liberating; it is sad that such a simple pleasure is so rare in modern life. Clocks are now a ubiquitous menace. Where the sun used to suffice, we now have our watches, phones, computers, and iPads perpetually reminding us what time it is and when we next need to do something. As clocks have become increasingly tyrannical, our lives have been chopped up into ever smaller slices of time. It's no wonder, then, that we cannot help but be focused on the short term.

Indeed, one easy way to build a good business these days is to get people what they want as quickly as possible. Click "buy," and Amazon will deliver almost anything you want or need to your doorstep within a day or two. Within a few years, Amazon will use "octocopter" drones to shorten the delivery time to 30 minutes. Because of the convenience it provides—and the speed with which it can deliver—Amazon has become one of the greatest and most successful modern companies. In the modern world, our desires can be quickly quenched. Patience was a twentieth-century virtue: we are the instant gratification generation.

Given Amazon's role as our primary instant-gratification engine, I was fascinated to learn that Amazon's founder Jeff Bezos had committed a significant amount of money to build a clock inside a mountain in West Texas that will last for 10,000 years and is meant to be an icon for long-term thinking. The clock will only tick once per year, the "minute" hand will tick once per century, and the cuckoo will only appear at each new millennium.[1] Reorienting people toward the long term is a difficult and admirable ambition, but one that Bezos considers very important. "As I see it, humans are now technologically advanced enough that we can create not only extraordinary wonders but also civilization-scale problems," says Bezos on the website promoting the project.[2] A long-term perspective like the one that the 10,000-year clock intends to promote is rare because our evolved biology makes us short sighted by nature. In a primitive setting, it is more important to focus on immediate needs and dangers rather than on long-term goals. How far into the future are you normally focused? For most, the future means days, weeks, and months—not years and decades. In the modern setting, this myopic focus is unhealthy, because short-term thinking can create long-term problems. This is especially true for investing, where, thanks to compounding, what we do in the present is magnified by time.

Most "investors" these days are speculators, meaning they make their decisions based on what they think will happen in the next few months or years rather than the next two or three decades. They make trades into and out of major asset classes, trying to guess what might work next. One amusing sign that we have become less strategic and more tactical is a popular ad on financial news networks at the moment. The ad shows a man in front of double computer monitors filled with price charts, pumping his fist after making a trade. No good investing decision should inspire that much excitement—but the ad plays well to our short-sighted instincts.

I'll admit that it is difficult to think long term. My investment horizon is well over 30 years, which is longer than I've been alive— and I don't remember anything before I was ten years old. Trying to think so far into the future poses many challenges, but it is well worth the effort. This chapter explores how we get in our own way when we focus on the short term and how to avoid doing so in the future. I'll explore the power of delaying gratification, show why we need to redefine "risk," and explain why the ability to think long-term gives individual investors advantage over professional investors.

Delayed Gratification

While instant gratification has become the norm, there is tremendous power in delaying gratification. The most famous study comparing short-term versus long-term rewards was first conducted by Walter Mischel in the early 1970s. Mischel tempted young children (between the ages of three and five) with tasty treats like cookies and marshmallows to see if the ability to delay gratification was related to other personality attributes that emerged later in the children's lives. A researcher would offer a single cookie to each child and tell them they could either eat the single cookie right away, or, if they could wait while the researcher left the room for 15 minutes or so, be rewarded with a second cookie. It's no surprise that many kids ate the treat right away (I know I would have), but some kids were able to wait to earn a double-cookie reward. Mischel followed these young children for decades, and found that the kids who were able to wait for the second cookie had much higher SAT scores, were more likely to complete college, were in better shape, and earned higher incomes than the kids who couldn't resist eating the first cookie right away.[3]

Most of us go for the first cookie. We are wired to prefer immediate rewards over distant rewards, even if the distant reward is much better than the immediate one. When it comes to money, this preference for instant gratification is a powerful force. We make irrational choices if it means we can get something we want right away. Many people would rather receive $100 today than $110 tomorrow because the $100 is an instant reward, but if you offer the same choices 30 days into the future, most would rather get $110 on day 31 than $100 on day 30.[4] We tend to make more rational choices when we are making similar comparisons for two future dates, but when the choice is between now and later, we consistently make stupid choices to get what we want now. We only choose a delayed reward over a current reward if we are getting a fantastic deal. To forgo $15 today, people require (on average) $30 in three months, $60 dollars in one year, and $100 in three years.[5] Requiring $60 in a year to forgo a $15 reward now equates to an annual 300 percent return, which never happens in the stock market. That we tend to require such outrageous future rewards in order to forgo an immediate reward is a major flaw with which investors must contend. We often make bad decisions to make ourselves feel good (or safe) in the moment at the expense of our long-term wealth.

The most amazing aspect of these now-versus-later errors is the various brain areas that are involved when we make short-sighted decisions (immediate rewards) and long-sighted decisions (future rewards). Our limbic system, the emotional center of our brain that we share with our mammalian cousins, drives us toward immediate rewards. But when test subjects opt instead for the future rewards, then their prefrontal cortex—the most advanced part of the brain—shows increased activation. The research that identified this phenomenon in our brains, conducted by Samuel McClure, provides hard evidence that our monkey brains dominate our decision making and bias us toward short-term rewards. As McClure says, "in economics, intertemporal choice has long been recognized as a domain in which 'the passions' can have a large sway in affecting our choices. Our findings lend support to this intuition."[6] Passions (i.e. emotions) dominate our decision making but we can make smarter decisions if we can keep our emotions in check. When making tough calls, try to think like Spock, not like Captain Kirk.

Now back to cookies and marshmallows. McClure's findings suggest that the kids who were able to choose future rewards had higher activity in their frontal cortices, while the kids that gobbled up the first cookie or marshmallow were slaves to their emotional, midbrain desires. Many kids who were able to take the long view used very funny strategies to distract themselves. Holly Palmeri and Celeste Kidd, who conducted a more recent version of the marshmallow study, said some kids danced in their seats, sang, took pretend naps, or nibbled a piece of the marshmallow so that it looked untouched. Another kid grabbed the marshmallow and sat on it to put it out of his mind.[7] Strategies for delaying gratification used by the kids in this experiment are applicable in markets, too. Kids just distracted themselves and ignored the marshmallows. We can also ignore and distract ourselves from short-term market fluctuations. We can check our portfolios much less often (once a year is fine), we can ignore the 24-hour news cycle, and we can remind ourselves that the most exciting stocks on any given day are often the most expensive. The difference between receiving one or two marshmallows is similar to spending now versus investing for the future. But thanks to compounding returns, by delaying gratification through investing you will end up with a far better reward than a couple of marshmallows.

Being self-aware is the first step toward correcting shortsighted behavior. When making any investment decision, you should ask yourself, "Am I taking this action because it will feel good now or because it will likely be good for my financial future?" A good rule of thumb is that any investment choice that feels good is a bad one, and anything that seems scary or boring is often a good one.

The key lesson here is that while we fancy ourselves to be very smart creatures, our thinking is still driven by our ancient mammalian, emotional midbrain. This midbrain pushes us toward instant gratification and we will never escape its influence; but if we can reorient ourselves toward the long term, using the most modern part of our brain—the rational prefrontal cortex—we can make decisions that result in much better long-term investing outcomes. The best way to convince ourselves to think further into the future is by redefining risk.

Risk Redefined

Following the 2008 global financial crisis, investors now care more about "risk" than they do about "return." Investments that claim to offer "down-side protection" sell like hotcakes, because everyone wants to avoid the pain that would come with another crash. Late in bull markets, people want growth, but after big bear markets like the one between 2007 and 2009, investors always prefer "low-risk" investments that will "preserve their wealth." But what does low risk really mean? Many investors think that a risky investment is one that bounces around a lot over short time periods. We hate to watch our portfolios drop by 10 percent or 20 percent in just three months or by 40 to 50 percent in a year. Cash or bonds will never have short returns that are that bad, so they seem much less risky.

But risk should not be defined as how volatile investments are in the short term. Risk is just the odds that each individual's long-term goals will not be achieved. Stocks are considered the most "risky" investment, at least relative to bonds and cash, because their returns are much more volatile. Stocks bounce around a lot more and have much more extreme best- and worst-case scenarios than do bonds or cash over short periods. But as the time period lengthens, stocks become less and less risky. There is a dangerous misperception that the best way to reduce risk is to own fewer stocks in one's portfolio and own more bonds and cash. That is what investors did in 2009—they sold stocks and bought bonds. They did so because risk is often defined in absolute terms—that is, stocks are riskier than bonds, period.

With risk defined as such, the easiest way to reduce it would be to own fewer stocks. But an absolute definition of risk makes no sense. It should instead be defined *relative* to each investor's time horizon. Stocks are indeed much riskier than bonds or cash over a one-year time horizon, but we don't have a one-year time horizon! When evaluated over 20 to 30 years—the luxurious time horizon that we millennials enjoy—the story is flipped. For long holding periods, stocks become by far the safest investment, and bonds and cash become very risky. Table 8.1 shows the percentage of time that stocks, bonds, and T-bills have negative real returns over holding periods between one month and 30 years, and Table 8.2 lists the absolute worst-case scenario for each asset class over the same intervals.[8]

In the short term, stocks are the riskiest assets by far. Between the summers of 1931 and 1932, in the heat of the Great Depression, stocks declined 64 percent in value in just

Table 8.1   Negative Real Return Frequency (% of Observations)

Time frame	S&P 500	Government bonds	T-Bills
1 month	40%	46%	39%
3 months	38%	44%	39%
1 year	31%	36%	38%
5 year	25%	40%	40%
10 year	15%	41%	38%
20 year	0%	49%	30%
30 year	0%	40%	39%

Source: Roger Ibbotson.

Table 8.2   Worst-Case Scenario

Time frame	S&P 500	Government bonds	T-bills
1 month	–29%	–12%	–6%
3 months	–43%	–18%	–9%
1 year	–64%	–28%	–16%
5 year	–51%	–45%	–28%
10 year	–45%	–49%	–42%
20 year	6%	–53%	–48%
30 year	236%	–52%	–43%

Source: Roger Ibbotson.

12 months. More recently, between February 2008 and February 2009, investors saw their stock portfolios drop an average of 43 percent. By contrast, the worst one-year period (after inflation) for bonds was minus 11.6 percent and minus 5.5 percent for T-bills—much more manageable short-term losses. But as the time horizons lengthen, stocks become safer and safer, and bonds and bills become riskier and riskier. While stocks lose real value in 31 percent of one-year periods, they have never lost money in any 20-year period. Bonds—a perceived safe haven— have negative real returns half of the time during 20-year

periods and 40 percent of the time in 30-year periods. Thanks to inflation, T-bills and bonds are often a bad choice over the long term.

We millennials must evaluate risk relative to our long-term horizon and try to ignore short-term volatility. Even if you'd invested in the stock market on the eve of the Great Depression in 1929—the single worst time to invest in the stock market in recorded history—you'd still have made money 20 years later. During the toughest times in the stock market, like 2000–2002 or 2007–2009, investors tend to trade long-term stock returns for the perceived short-term protection of cash and bonds—but this is backward! If anything, we should snatch up stocks during market crashes, because that is when they go on sale. As Ben Graham said, "bear markets are when stocks return to their rightful owners."

Millennial Money Risk

Any strategy designed to outperform the market carries a second kind of risk—that it will underperform the stock market as a whole. The Millennial Money strategy appears risky over the short term, but is much safer than the overall market over the long term. Figure 8.1 shows the excess return (above or below the market) earned through the Millennial Money strategy over the very short term (one month) and very long term (20 years). The story told by Figure 8.1 is similar to the comparison between stocks and bonds or cash: risky in the short term, but safe in the long term.

There are many months (the darker, jagged line in Figure 8.1) when the strategy loses to the market by more than 3 percent, and some months where it loses by as much as 5 percent. While they aren't shown in Figure 8.1, there are even year-long periods when the Millennial Money strategy underperforms by more than

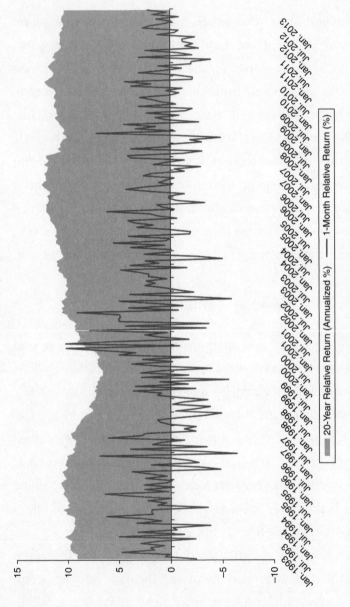

Figure 8.1 Short-Term and Long-Term Excess Returns. Millennial Money strategy vs. market

20 percent. For the strategies that I manage at my day job, short-term underperformance always triggers calls from clients who want to know what is happening to their portfolios. It is difficult to live through short bursts of underperformance, but the story changes when we evaluate the same relative returns over 20-year periods. As Emerson said, "the years teach much which the days never know." The worst case scenario over any 20-year period was *outperformance* of 6.5 percent per year. Even in the worst 20-year periods, the Millennial Money strategy has delivered strong excess returns. This is why risk must be tied to a time horizon. For our generation, stocks are the least risky asset class, and building unique portfolios is the least risky way to buy stocks.

The more you check the news or check your portfolio, the more likely you are to lose your long-term perspective. Remember that the news is often a perfect contrary indicator. On March 9, 2009—the exact market bottom following the recent global financial crisis—*Time* magazine's cover showed a picture of two hands grasping a frayed rope; the cover said, HOLDING ON FOR DEAR LIFE. If you had money in the stock market, it was already worth half what it used to be, and *Time*'s cover made it easy to worry that more bad news lay ahead.

Paul Andreassen, a researcher at Harvard University, conducted a study to learn what impact the news has on people's investing decisions. He had subjects manage portfolios with the same hypothetical stocks. Each portfolio started half in cash and half in stocks, and the only instruction given was that subjects should buy low and sell high—earning the best returns they could over the trial period. Everyone was shown price trends for the stocks available to buy and sell, but the twist on the study was that one group was also given news stories for their stocks—which they were told came from the *Wall Street Journal*. The other group received no news whatsoever. The subjects who saw no news followed the appropriate strategy: they tended to buy low and sell high. But the subjects who read the news stories traded too often and had portfolios that performed considerably worse than the subjects who were given no news. Even more enlightening, the worst performance for the news group came when stock prices were highly volatile.[9] Since it is our nature to watch more news during periods of extreme volatility, this study serves as a great reminder that paying too much attention to stock market news can spell doom for your portfolio. News is almost never helpful— you will never read a story in the *Wall Street Journal* whose headline reads MARKET POISED TO DELIVER STRONG RETURNS OVER THE NEXT 30 YEARS.

Isaac Asimov wrote that "it is the invariable lesson to humanity that distance in time lends focus. It is not recorded, incidentally, that the lesson has ever been permanently learned." The key lesson to be taken from this section is that short-term returns for stocks, and short-term *excess* returns for the Millennial Money strategy, can appear very risky but they are random. As much as we want to find meaning in these short-term movements, there is usually none to be found.

In 2013, the market continued a rather remarkable bull run, and was up 130 percent from the March 2009 low.[10] Sadly, investors were just then starting to buy stocks again, having missed an amazing five-year opportunity. This happened because they were too worried about "risk." If they had defined risk differently, then what looked like a calamity would have been viewed as an opportunity. At some point in the next several years, we will likely see yet another frightening decline in stock prices—it may even be happening as this book goes to print. The market will do its best to scare you out of stocks. When that happens, remember that while stocks have had many terrible one-year returns, they've never had a negative 20-year return.

Fake Patterns Everywhere

We think that we can make sense of the market's short-term fluctuations because our brains are pattern junkies. When we see two of something, we then expect a third. Recognizing patterns is an important cognitive survival tool, but false pattern recognition leads us astray in markets. We tend to extrapolate very recent trends too far into the future, and then make decisions based on these biased long-term expectations.

In his book *Your Money & Your Brain*, Jason Zweig, one of my favorite writers on all things investing, documented a hilarious example of our pattern-hungry brains being fooled by randomness.[11] In the study he summarizes, people were pitted against pigeons in a pattern detection game, and the pigeons won. Both human and bird-brained participants were shown two lights, one red and one green, which were flashed 20 times per round. The flashing lights were rigged such that the green one flashed 80 percent of the time, but beyond the 80 percent rule, the exact sequence was random. The human and bird participants were asked to guess which light would flash next, and would receive a reward if correct. The pigeons quickly figured out that the green light flashed more often and that the best strategy was just to guess green every time. By doing so, the pigeons' average score was about 80 percent. But humans—convinced that they could glean some other pattern in the random sequences—would try to outsmart the random lights by sometimes guessing red. The result: humans only got it right 68 percent of the time.

Making matters worse, our pattern-hungry brains are also biased toward very recent trends. Individual and professional investors alike project current circumstances too far into the future and make predictions that are heavily influenced by the recent past. We've already seen how individual investors routinely buy and sell mutual funds at the wrong time—buying after the market has done well and selling after it has done poorly. Professional academic forecasters make the same mistake. In a survey conducted by Ivo Welch in the late 1990s—near the technology bubble's peak—several hundred academics were asked to estimate the amount by which stocks would beat bonds over the coming 30 years. In the heat of the stock market bubble, their average estimate was 7.2 percent per year.[12] But when they were surveyed again in 2001, after the market had crashed, their estimate was *lower* than before, coming in at 5.5 percent. Of 426 academics polled in the second survey, just 58 (14 percent) were bullish in 2001. Again this is backward because you should be the most bullish *after* a crash, not before. In 2001, the very recent crash was a negative influence on their very long-term predictions about the market, just as the bull market was a positive influence just a few years earlier.[13]

This bias that we have toward the recent past when forming predictions about the future happens because of some intriguing brain chemistry. The neurotransmitter dopamine plays a large role in memory, because dopamine surges help us learn. As J. Madeline Nash describes it, "at a purely chemical level, every experience humans find enjoyable—whether listening to music, embracing a lover or savoring chocolate—amounts to little more than an explosion of dopamine in the nucleus accumbens, as exhilarating and ephemeral as a firecracker."[14] Because we are rewarded with these surges, we learn to partake more in whatever activity it was that caused the dopamine explosion. It is incredible, then, that the signals from dopamine neurons fade over time, meaning that neurons associated with more recent events fire stronger and therefore have a disproportionally high influence on our predictions for the future.[15] Our dopamine reward system creates an equation in our brains for predicting the future and, in the equation, more recent experiences are more important than older experiences. Ideally, when analyzing markets and making predictions about the future, we'd place an equal emphasis or weight on all the evidence we had about market movements over their long history—but our brains orient us to the recent past when making predictions about the future. The key lesson is that if you think you've spotted a short-term trend in the market, you've probably been duped. Ignore impulses to act on current trends, because they are probably imaginary and/or temporary.

Individual Investor Edge

There is one final aspect of long-term thinking that is very important for young investors. Because we are bombarded with stories about how difficult it is to beat the market, you may feel as though you can't beat the market or the professionals over the long term. When I first started in the business, it seemed like the pros had an enormous edge over small individual investors. Many professionals that I met had earned their masters degrees in things like financial mathematics, had PhDs in economics, had studied 1,000 hours to earn their chartered financial analyst (CFA) designation, and had studied under experienced portfolio managers. But I learned that professionals, despite all their training and resources, have one huge disadvantage—they are beholden to their bosses and their clients, and their jobs are on the line when they perform poorly in the short term. To minimize their "career risk," professionals make decisions that sacrifice large potential long-term rewards in favor of more secure short-term returns, or at least returns that are

similar to the overall market. I've focused on 20- to 50-year investment horizons in this book because that is what millennials should
focus on. But in professional investing, three years is an eternity. If
a professional manager is losing to the market for three years running, he will often be fired and replaced with another professional
manager, usually one that has done well in the past three years.

Clients evaluate managers' performance at least once a quarter
and sometimes once a month. These short time periods are mean-
ingless in the market, but have become the standard for measuring
performance. We've had many clients hire us and then threaten to
fire us less than one year later because we've underperformed. This
concern about short-term performance has repercussions up and
down the money management business. Money managers want
to do well for their clients (which can be individuals, institutions,
pension plans, endowments, or foundations), but they also want to
keep their jobs. If they underperform the market, or as a pension
manager they hire managers that underperform the market, there
is a good chance that they will be fired. Making bold decisions
introduces "career risk," because it increases the chances that their
decisions will get them canned.

Sadly, lowering career risk also leads to lower returns. Many
professional money managers have adopted a style known as
"closet indexing," so-called because their portfolios are so similar
to the overall market that they might as well be an index fund. This
lowers career risk because closet indexers won't have years where
they lose badly to the market. But we've already learned that being
different is the real key to long-term success, so closet indexers also
fail to beat the market by much. Once you account for their fees,
these closet indexers aren't worth hiring. The percentage of managers who are closet indexers varies by country, but most countries
have a rather large percentage. In Canada, 37 percent of assets

were with closet indexers in 2010.[16] Several European countries have a closet indexing problem as well. Thirty-two percent of assets in the United Kingdom, 29 percent in France, and a whopping 56 percent in Sweden are invested with closet index managers. The United States is unique because it has among the highest percentages of indexed money (27 percent) but among the lowest levels of closet indexed money (15 percent).[17] Closet indexing may help professional managers reduce their career risk, but they do so at the expense of their investors, who are paying active management fees for index-like returns. Across all 32 countries studied, the total annual costs to shareholders for true index funds is 0.35 percent, but the cost to shareholders of closet index funds is 1.64 percent. This is a huge cost for an index-like fund, and is barely lower than costs for funds that *are* different from the market, which cost an average of 1.66 percent. With such high fees, closet indexers have underperformed the market over time. Individual investors don't have this problem, because individuals don't have to worry about being fired for a bad year's performance.

Another group that acts to reduce career risk includes plan sponsors—the people managing pension funds, endowments, and foundations. One way they manage career risk is to fire managers who have underperformed in the last few years and hire those that have performed well. When I was a kid my parents would tell me that we could do things the easy way or the hard way (ever the contentious contrarian, I'd often choose the hard way). Chasing recent performance is investing the easy way. It's very easy to fire managers that are performing poorly and hire those that have done well in the recent past, because as humans we expect recent trends to continue. But a fascinating study confirmed that these hiring and firing decisions tend to be ill-fated. Amit Goyal and Sunil Wahal studied 3,400 different plan sponsors who made 9,000 hiring and firing decisions over a ten-year period. They found that managers being hired had outperformed the market by 3 percent on average, and that the number one reason for firing a manager was because they underperformed. Unfortunately for the plan sponsors, the managers hired went on to underperform the market (after fees), while many that they fired went on to outperform the managers that they hired![18]

There are two key lessons here for the individual investor. First, even if the sophistication of professional managers makes it seem as though individual investors do not have an edge, they do. Without a job to worry about, individual investors can tolerate short-term underperformance on the path to long-term outperformance. Second, if you are to hire a professional manager (look for one that uses a strategy similar to the Millennial Money strategy), make sure that they aren't a closet indexer charging active management fees. Find mutual funds or ETFs that are very different from the market.

A Long-Term Mind-set

Whenever you feel the urge to do something with your portfolio because of what is going on in the market at the moment, ask yourself this question: looking back on this decision in ten years, will you believe that you made this decision for your long-term financial well-being or will you believe that you made the decision in response to short-term market circumstances? To imagine looking back on a decision sometime in the future can lend valuable perspective to a current decision. This question can also help you untangle yourself from the market's mood. I am a junkie for Eastern philosophy and think that many core Eastern ideas—many of them thousands of years old—serve well as pearls of market wisdom. In a collection of the Buddha's sayings called the *Dhammapada*, the Buddha tells us, "Do not give your attention to what others do or fail to do; give it to what you do or fail to do." So much short-term behavior results when investors get caught up in the moment and caught up in what everyone else is doing and thinking. Don't worry about what the market thinks or what the experts think. Worry about whether your behavior is good for you, and remember just how long an investing future you have ahead of you.

In the stock market, all news, crazes, and stock prices are temporary and transitory. Abraham Lincoln told the story of "an Eastern monarch [who] once charged his wise men to invent him a sentence to be ever in view, and which should be true and appropriate in all times and situations. They presented him the words, 'And this too, shall pass away.' How much it expresses! How chastening in the hour of pride! How consoling in the depths of affliction!" What Lincoln recognized in this simple phrase can be applied to our investing decisions. It is essential that in our hours of pride (and greed) and during our depths of affliction (and fear) we remind ourselves: this too shall pass. Ignore the news, ignore the experts, and remember that your long-time horizon gives you an edge over many professionals. In the stock market, time and patience are the most powerful warriors.

As you build your portfolios over the years, you will face many scary and many exciting markets that will make you want to sell in panic or buy in greed. Greed and fear, the push and the pull, are the two most destructive forces that we will face. They have ruined more portfolios than any market crash. They are the two strongest emotional influences that live in the short term—the here-and-now. The next chapter discusses the middle way between these two emotional extremes, and why you must avoid the perils of both the push and the pull.

9

THE PUSH AND THE PULL

One of the great privileges of my life was a visit to the Okavango Delta and the Kalahari Desert in Botswana. Thinking back on the trip, two different bush walks stand out in my memory. The first was with a group of Kalahari Bushmen, one of the few remaining traditional peoples of Africa. As my family and I walked through the desert with them, all I saw was dirt and dead grass. But the hyper-aware Bushmen quickly spotted signs of food, tracks, opportunities, and dangers. It was fascinating to watch these wonderful people navigate their landscape. Having honed their natural abilities, they were well suited to exist and thrive in their environment. Walking with them made me realize that in modern cities, human beings are like fish out of water, because we use very few of our innate abilities. My first lesson was that our brains are well developed for the bush.

The second walk was through the Okavango Delta where lions, charging elephants, and hippos pose a constant and potentially fatal threat. Even though we weren't in any real danger—our walking guide had an oversized rifle—I was amazed by how much more vigilant and focused we immediately became. We'd all spent our lives without facing any real predatory threats, but everyone's awareness was heightened. Every detail mattered: staying upwind so as not to alarm animals with our scent, staying near cover, staying close together, and being quiet. It was an exhilarating feeling, even though we didn't come across anything more threatening than some fast-moving elephants. What stood out from this second walk was the great care that we took to avoid any danger. We even made sure to avoid doing anything that might increase the odds of danger. The fear we felt was both useful and necessary.

There are not many groups of traditional people like the Kalahari Bushmen left in the world, but the few groups that do remain provide a glimpse into our past. One common trait of traditional people is their cautiousness. For our species to survive, being extra careful has been a good thing. Anthropologist Jared Diamond has spent decades with the traditional people of New Guinea and has written extensively about his travels. On one trip to the forest with New Guinea companions, Diamond chose a giant mossy tree to camp under for the night. But to his surprise, his friends refused to camp there because, as they explained, the tree was dead and might fall and kill them as they slept. At first, Diamond thought this was a gross overreaction because the tree hadn't even begun to rot. But in the weeks and months that followed he realized that trees fall quite often in the forest, and therefore do pose a threat to the New Guinea people who spend 100 nights a year sleeping there. As they saw it, even a low-probability threat was best avoided: better safe than sorry. Diamond calls this hyperprudent behavior "constructive paranoia." The behavior seems paranoid because the odds of something bad happening are low, but constructive because by being so vigilant in many ways, people like Diamond's New Guinea friends significantly extend their life expectancy.[1]

In the modern world, we face threats like cars, accidents, and alcohol—and if we get hit by a car or fall off a ladder, we have doctors to fix us up. In stark contrast, the top threats faced by the Kalahari !Kung tribe are, in order: poisoned arrows, fire, large animals (lions, elephants, and hippos), poisonous snakes, a fall from a tree, infected thorn scratches, getting lost, and lightning.[2] The !Kung are overly sensitive to these threats and will take extreme measures to protect themselves from them. Constructive paranoia works—and it contributes to our evolutionary fitness.

In the stock market, however, constructive paranoia works against us. Thanks to our evolutionary legacy, we are about twice as sensitive to financial losses as we are to financial gains—a tendency that skews our behavior and diminishes our returns. We are sensitive to fear, but greed also affects our investing behavior in dangerous ways. The most important decisions we will make as investors will be at emotional stock-market extremes, in markets characterized by excitement and greed, or in those characterized by fear and panic. It is during these times that we must make sure that rational thought prevails and that we stick to our long-term strategy. This means doing nothing when it feels like we must do *something*. In the market, greed inspires behavior that looks psychotic in hindsight, and fear routinely camouflages the best opportunities. Fear motivates us more than greed, but both intense emotions have ruined many investors. This chapter explores how greed and fear create traps for investors and what to look for in the market to identify these traps ahead of time, and thereby avoid their snare.

While the research in this chapter may strike you as obvious, most of our understanding of the investor psyche is very new. The godfathers of behavioral finance—Daniel Kahneman and Amos Tversky—published their first major research on the topic in 1979, right around the time that the first millennials were born.[3] This research represents another huge edge for our generation because to get out of our own way we need to know where and when we are likely to screw up. Human nature doesn't change, so our emotions will tempt us into foolish decisions just like they have all previous generations, but we have the advantage of knowing just how systematically wrong our intuitions tend to be.

Fear in the Brain

Like the Bushmen, we are wired more for avoiding danger than approaching rewards. We tend to identify potential threats by detecting patterns, but we often make errors and see patterns where none exist; this makes us overly cautious. Michael Shermer, author of *The Mind of the Market*, classifies our pattern detection errors as either type I or type II. A type I error is when we think we see a threat and take action to escape, but it turns out to be nothing. We may think, for example, that a rustle in the bush is a lurking lion, but it's just the wind. Type I errors are like behavioral insurance policies. We may act overly careful after the wind rustles the grass, but on the off chance there is a lion there, we have increased our odds of survival by taking caution. A type II error, by contrast, is thinking that the rustle in the grass is just the wind, when in fact it's a lion. Type II errors are much more dangerous and costly because they leave us defenseless against potentially fatal threats.

You can see how evolution would favor type I errors over type II errors, since type I errors were more likely to ensure our survival. As a result, our brains are wired to respond faster and stronger to negative experiences than to positive ones. This negativity bias is ubiquitous. We respond more quickly to fearful facial expressions than we do to neutral or happy expressions,[4] and even if we don't consciously see the fearful expressions, our brain's fear center (the amygdala) still lights up.[5] If you want a happy spouse or significant other, researchers have identified that for a healthy relationship you need five good interactions for every bad one.[6] This negativity bias goes by another name in the stock market—loss aversion—and is perhaps the most dangerous bias that we face as investors. Loss aversion was first studied by Nobel laureate Daniel Kahneman, whose book *Thinking, Fast and Slow* is my all-time favorite book on psychology.[7] Along with his long-time research partner, the late Amos Tversky, Kahneman discovered that losing $100 is about as painful as winning $200 is pleasurable. This imbalance makes perfect sense because our sensitivity to losses, and our tendency to make type I errors rather than type II errors, is baked into our brains. As neuroscientist Rick Hanson says, "When an event is flagged as negative, the hippocampus makes sure it's stored carefully for future reference. Once burned, twice shy. Your brain is like Velcro for negative experiences and Teflon for positive ones—even though most of your experiences are probably neutral or positive."[8] We millennials have already been burned by the stock, job, and housing markets, so it's no surprise that we are wary of risk.

Loss aversion has a huge impact on our investing decisions, especially during bear markets and near market bottoms. If we were rational, we'd buy near market bottoms when prices are low, but loss aversion pulls us away from the market. One fascinating study sheds light on people's behavior after experiencing a loss. In the study, led by researcher Baba Shiv from Stanford University, participants played an investment game where each was given $20 to start and asked to make 20 separate $1 investment decisions. In each round, their options were to "invest" or to "not invest." If they chose not to invest they kept their dollar and moved on to the next round. If they chose to invest their dollar, the outcome was determined by a coin toss. If the coin landed on heads, the participant would lose their dollar, but if it came up tails, they would receive $2.50. The most profitable strategy in this game would be to play every round, because every dollar invested has a $1.25 expected value (50 percent times $2.50).

The twist in the study was that one group of participants had suffered brain damage which affected key emotional centers in the brain such as the amygdala or the insula. The other participants had either no brain damage at all or brain damage which affected brain areas not associated with emotion. The results were stunning. The participants with "normal" brains invested just 58 percent of the time, ending with $22.80 on average, but participants *with* brain damage to the amygdala and insula outperformed their healthy counterparts by 14.5 percent, investing 84 percent of the time and ending with an average of $25.70. Those with normal brains did so poorly due to their irrational behavior following a loss. Instead of recognizing the positive expected value of choosing "invest," the normal group was scared to lose twice in a row (loss aversion), so they invested *just 41 percent of the time after a loss*. For normal investors, emotions often trump rational thought. The brain-impaired group, meanwhile, were not affected by their losses and maintained their strategy, investing 85 percent of the time after losing on a prior coin flip.[9]

This may seem like a quaint example until you consider what real investors have done with their money since the March 2009 market low. Bonds are similar to the "don't invest" or safe option in Shiv's study, and stocks are similar to the "invest" option. We have seen that over time stocks consistently beat bonds, but after losses investors tend to avoid investing in stocks. Figure 9.1 shows that since the market bottom, investors have *bought* almost $1 trillion dollars worth of "safe" bond funds, and *sold* nearly $200 billion of their "risky" stock funds. But during that time period

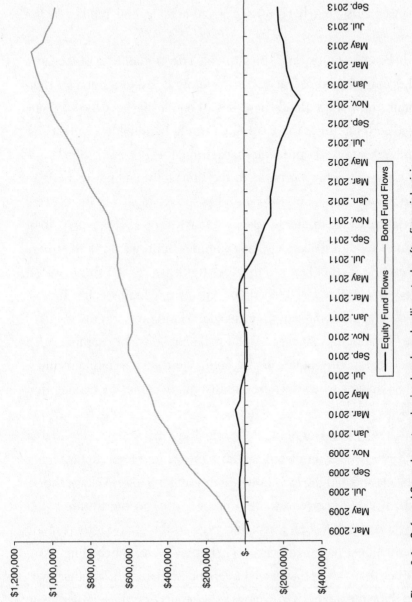

Figure 9.1   Safe and Sorry. Investors buying bonds and selling stocks after financial crisis

Source: Fund flows from Investment Company Institute

(between March 2009 and September 2013), the stock market gained 130 percent, while the bond market grew just 16 percent.[10] Investors tried to play it safe—just like the "normal" brain study participants—but have missed a remarkable bull market in the process.

People opt for "safe" investments *after* a market crash because the combination of fear and uncertainty is just too much for their brains to handle. Bonds have been popular because they are safe *and* certain: unless there is a rare default, bondholders will receive interest and their principle back from the borrower. Stocks are the opposite—they are risky in the short term and always have an uncertain future (any stock could go to zero or soar to unexpected heights). Many studies have shown that we cope better with pain or punishment if we know what's coming. But if we think that more pain (like further losses in the stock market) *might* lie ahead, we get very uncomfortable. Uncertainty drives our brains crazy and we will go to irrational lengths to avoid it. Hating uncertainty is part of our evolutionary lineage. Alpha male baboons, for example, keep their competition guessing by being aggressive at random times. Not knowing when the next outburst might come, the competition is kept at bay.[11]

It's the same for humans. In one study, many people faced with the prospect of an electric shock were willing to accept a higher voltage shock right away rather than wait for a lower voltage shock, which would arrive at some unknown time in the future. fMRI brain scans show that the pain centers in the brain for these study participants lit up the most when they were anticipating pain, rather than when they were experiencing pain.[12] In another twist on the same theme, participants experienced less stress if they knew that they would receive 20 intense shocks than if they knew that they would receive 17 mild shocks with 3 intense shocks coming at random times. Not knowing when an intense shock might come, people sweated more and had higher heart rates than those that *knew* they'd receive an intense shock every time.[13] We are often happy to suffer more now if we know that we won't have to suffer later.

The same held true for investors buying bonds like hot cakes for four years after the financial crisis of 2008. Neuroscientist Robert Sapolsky writes,

> A frequent myth in both cognitive science and economics is that we go about trying to understand causality in a logical way. But instead, that gleaming, sensible cortex sits there marinating in all sorts of frothy, hormonal, affective influences, and that can make for rational assessments being pretty irrational. And thus we wind up finding the chance of punishment to be more stressful than the certainty of punishment. And on the flip side, if the lottery payoff is big enough, we decide that we've got the lucky number, no matter what the odds, and we're soon going to be in social grooming heaven.[14]

At both market extremes, our brains trick us into acting a fool.

Before the Boom Come Doom and Gloom

The best investors are able to overcome fear, uncertainty, and discomfort. In fact, doom and gloom are often the best sign of a buying opportunity (2009 was the perfect example). This is true for individual stocks and for the market as a whole. One of author Joseph Campbell's maxims holds true for the stock market: "The cave you fear to enter holds the treasure you seek."

When investors are forecasting doom and gloom for stocks, it shows up in their valuations. We've already seen that cheaper stocks (with lower expectations) perform much better than the market, but the same is true for the market as a whole. The best way to measure the market's valuation is through the ten-year price-to-earnings ratio. This takes the average earnings for an entire market over the prior ten-year period and compares them to today's price. Nobel laureate Robert Schiller has calculated this ratio all the way back to 1881. When the ratio for the overall market is high (expensive, high expectations), returns over the next ten years tend to be weak, and when the ratio is low (cheap, low expectations), returns tend to be strong.

When you can buy the S&P 500 for less than 15 times earnings, the average future returns over the *next* ten years are 11.9 percent per year, which is a good deal higher than the normal 8.8 percent return for the market.[15] But when you pay more than 25 times earnings, the average future ten-year returns are just 2.5 percent per year. Greed and fear help set the market's P/E ratio: when the market is priced at less than 15 times earnings, people tend to be fearful and pessimistic about the future, whereas when the market is priced higher than 25 times earnings, people are greedy and optimistic. Major lows for the ten-year P/E ratio were in 1921, 1982, and 2009—all peak periods of extreme doom and gloom in the stock market, but also the starting points for the most impressive bull markets in history. The absolute tops in valuation, by contrast, have been 1901, 1929, 1966, and 2000—all euphoric times that preceded brutal bear markets.

The Shiller P/E ratio was a relevant measure in September 2013, because the S&P 500 was trading at 25 times earnings—much higher than normal. This high valuation sounds gloomy, but it also highlights why investors in America should diversify their portfolios to hold more global stocks. In late 2013, the United States had the highest ten-year P/E ratio of any country in the developed world. Countries like France, the United Kingdom,

Brazil, and Italy all had ten-year P/Es less than 15. Greece, one of the world's scariest markets, was priced at just 4 times ten-year earnings.[16] Even if the US market remains expensive, there will always be markets around the world that are much cheaper. The higher P/E in the United States also means that there is a good chance that there will be a bear market in the next five years that will serve as the first test of millennials' long-term resolve. The ten-year P/E isn't the only way to measure valuation, but it shows us, once again, that the less you pay for stocks the more you will earn from them.

Greed in the Brain

While fear is the more powerful motivator, greed must also be tamed, because it can lead us into investments that can decimate our portfolios. Thanks to the fMRI brain scanner, we know which parts of the brain activate when we are anticipating and experiencing financial gains. It turns out that the activation pattern in our brains when we are experiencing financial gains is indistinguishable from brain patterns observed during other favorite human past times: cocaine use and sex.[17] No one should make investing decisions while high on cocaine (or while having sex for that matter), but that is analogous to what is happening when we chase after greed-driven market bubbles.

In December 2013, the Mega Millions jackpot reached its second highest level ever, with a $648,000,000 jackpot. My family and I were so seduced by this massive jackpot that we spent a dinner discussing what we'd do if we won. My sister and her husband even bought a few tickets, because to revel in the anticipation of a potential win seemed worth the price. I didn't buy a ticket, but I had to fight off the urge! Our brains do this to us all the time: they are wired to reward us with rushes of pleasure when we are anticipating rewards. When we think we might win a huge reward, we are pushed toward behavior that might help us capture it.

When we feel pleasure, it is because dopamine is flooding our brains—the same chemical that makes drugs feel so good. Tracking dopamine release in the brain is a great way to measure how much a brain values a certain reward. Greed is just like fear because it is during the anticipation phase that we are the most prone to act: the largest dopamine surges do not come once we have received a reward, but rather when we see some cue that a reward may be possible if we perform certain behaviors. In one study, monkeys were trained to expect a food reward after a light went on, but only if they pulled a lever several times. When their dopamine levels were monitored, the peak levels came right after the light went on but *before the monkey had pulled the lever.*[18] The reward itself was a letdown in comparison to the anticipation of the reward. Most people can relate: some relationships just aren't as fun after the thrill of the chase has subsided or been rewarded.

This evolved, neurochemical strategy makes sense: if our brains didn't promote the behavior itself, we'd never get any rewards. In the stock market, the chance for a quick reward is enticing, but the outcome is never a sure thing. When faced with potential rewards, uncertainty *increases* the amount of dopamine that floods our brains. Going back to the monkey experiment, where the sequence is light→dopamine rush→lever pull→reward. If the reward comes 50 percent of the time—perfect uncertainty—dopamine levels are higher than if the reward comes 75 percent of the time or 100 percent of the time. More uncertainty, more dopamine. As Robert Sapolsky points out, "this explains why intermittent reinforcements can be so profoundly reinforcing. And why the chance of a huge reward, even the most ludicrously remote [chance], can be so addictive, spiraling wild-eyed gamblers into squandering the kids' food money in the casino."[19] The brain systems that motivate greedy stock-market behavior should be ignored because you will feel the best right before you buy into a bubble, trying to earn a reward but exposing yourself to danger instead. If you can remember that this is true every time you feel pulled in by some alluring market story, you can stop yourself from making big blunders in your portfolio.

Greedy and Overconfident

Greed is compounded by the fact that we humans are overconfident. When polled, one group of entrepreneurs believed that the odds that their business would survive for five years were 81 percent, and one-third of those polled said their odds were 100 percent. Respondents were less optimistic about other businesses in the same field, giving them a 60 percent chance of survival. Sadly, the real five-year survival rate for new businesses is just 35 percent.[20] When people have an influence over any outcome, be it a small business or a portfolio, they tend to think they are much better than they are. When people are thinking about getting rich, it is easy to convince themselves that they are making a smart investment or that they can make a quick buck and get out before the market bubble bursts.

Bubbles recur throughout history, and the result is always the same. As President Harry Truman said, "The only new thing in the world is the history you don't know." Every bubble begins with a convincing story and is then fueled by greed and the dream of imminent riches. It would take perfect timing to profit from a bubble, but as people's brains are flooded with pleasure as they make more and more money, leaving the party early is nearly impossible. No matter the period in history, no matter the country or the story, asset bubbles all look the same.

The South Sea Bubble of 1720 was the first catastrophic market bubble. Between January 1 and July 1, 1720, South Sea stock rose by 640 percent. Because so many people were getting rich in South Sea stock, other stocks began to skyrocket as well. The Old East India Company, Million Bank, and the Royal African Company were all up more than 100 percent in just six months; Royal African was up 504 percent.[21] At its momentary peak, the London Stock Exchange—fueled by the South Sea Bubble—was worth more than five times the value of all the cash in Europe. The South Sea stock quickly collapsed, ending the year about where it started. When I first read about the South Sea Bubble, I remember thinking that most investors at the time just didn't have a clue. Clearly, I thought, they knew nothing about the company's operations and were just speculating. Surely a bubble as insane as South Sea couldn't happen in the modern world filled with easy access to information and thousands of investment analysts. Wrong! Since 1980, when the first millennials were born, this same cycle of greed, herding, bubble, and collapse has popped up at least five times. We've seen bubbles in the Japanese Nikkei Index, technology stocks, real estate, gold, and even Bitcoin. Figure 9.2 shows the meteoric rise and fall of all five.

The Nikkei, NASDAQ, gold, and Bitcoin all rose more than fivefold in five years, while real estate more than doubled. Bitcoin rose 11-fold in just 120 days! As I write, Bitcoin and gold are still in the midst of their crashes, and I hesitate to include them because the cases for their continued rise are compelling. Anything is possible, but a further crash is probable. Already in our lifetimes, the market has laid five deadly snares—and each ruined many

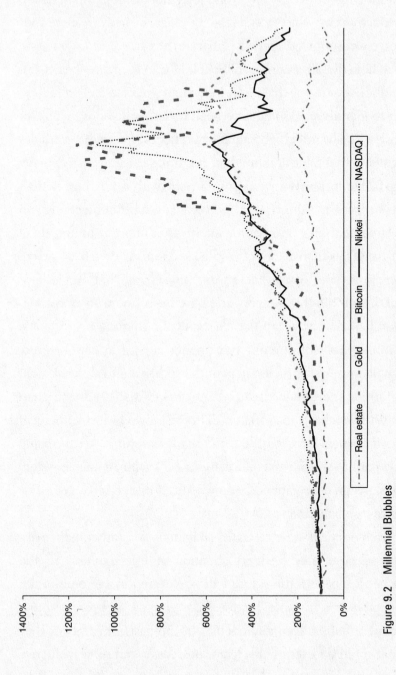

Figure 9.2   Millennial Bubbles

Source: Global Financial Data (Real Estate, Gold, Nikkei, NASDAQ) and bitcoincharts.org (Bitcoin)

investors. We will see many more similar market snares over our investing lifetimes. Any time you see a parabolic price chart tied to a seductive story (and several reactive magazine covers), close your eyes, cover your ears, and check back in a year.

These five are examples of bubbles for an entire asset class, but greed drives crazy behavior in individual stocks as well. The best way to identify stocks that have been fueled by greed is to look for those with absurdly high valuations. The most extreme examples are stocks that trade at more than 100 times earnings. It's virtually impossible to justify investing in a stock with a P/E higher than 100 because it requires that the company have tremendous and sustained earnings growth for many years into the future; these are truly speculative stocks, and speculation is driven by greed. Sometimes speculative stocks work out—Google and Apple have both fallen into this category and have been two of the most successful stocks of the last decade. Sadly, finding the next Google or Apple that will multiply your money is hard to do. For every Google and Apple, there are countless other high P/E stocks that perform horribly. Indeed, since 1963, stocks with a P/E higher than 100 have barely beaten inflation. They've grown by just 5.1 percent per year since 1963—just half the market's return over the same time period. When you come across a stock with an amazing story and sky-high expectations, remind yourself that you may get lucky, but you probably won't.

Bubbles will be especially dangerous for millennial investors, because they feed off attention and recognition in the media. Bubbles in the future will be covered in more news stories, promoted in more Twitter endorsements, and receive more overall attention than any bubbles in the past. This means they could build up even more steam, post faster and more seductive gains, and ultimately deliver quicker and more crippling crashes.

Investors used to read *Barron's* once a week; now they might see fifty Bitcoin stories in a day. Hype is investor kryptonite, and there is more of it than ever.

The Middle Way

It is hard to admit that we are just like everybody else and that we will make the same mistakes as countless investors before us. As Joseph Campbell wrote,

> generally we refuse to admit within ourselves the fullness of that pushing, self-protective, malodorous, carnivorous, lecherous fever which is the very nature of the organic cell. Rather, we tend to perfume, whitewash, and reinterpret; meanwhile imagining that all the flies in the ointment, all the hairs in the soup, are the faults of some unpleasant someone else.[22]

Remember that nature doesn't care how we survive, only that we do. Greed and fear will always make us want to do *something* with our portfolios because there will always be bubbles and panics, seductive stories, and scary headlines. Whenever you feel greed or fear creeping up in your brain, remember this old Zen joke, "Don't just do something, sit there!" I can think of no better market advice when you are feeling emotional.

It's impossible to control our desires, but we can learn to ignore them. We will never escape our constructive paranoia, and therefore we will try to avoid losses even if it is irrational to do so. The stock market's cycle of boom and bust does not mix well with our constructive paranoia or with our reward-seeking behavior. John Templeton offered the most concise description: "Bull markets are born on pessimism, grow on skepticism, mature on optimism, and die on euphoria. The time of maximum pessimism is the best time to buy, and the time of maximum optimism is the best time to sell." Being contrary has worked well for many famous investors but it is a psychologically painful thing to do. Most investors lack the intestinal fortitude to invest at or near market bottoms. But if you stick to your plan of automatic and regular contributions, you will, by default, buy near bottoms at cheaper prices. You will succeed by following the middle way between greed and fear, by being as dispassionate as you can be when the market is repelling you or enticing you. Recognizing, and then ignoring, these powerful influences will protect your portfolio and allow the market to do its work.

10

OPPORTUNITY KNOCKS

When opportunity knocks we must answer the call. Yet the long-term nature of our financial opportunity complicates things, because it is difficult to think decades ahead and harder still to take action with such a distant future in mind. Still, the potential reward is worth the effort. The more time we spend in the stock market, the better our results will be. There is no substitute for time, which means there is no investing advantage like youth. Warren Buffett, as a precocious boy, bought his first shares at age 11 and became a millionaire by age 32. We think of him as the world's richest and most brilliant investor, but he did not become a billionaire until 1990, when he was 60 years old. Perhaps the most important of his famous sayings is "someone's sitting in the shade today because someone planted a tree a long time ago." Imagine if he had started investing at 40. Even with his considerable talents, he may have just reached billionaire status in his 80s or never reached it at all. He would have been just one of many successful investors. Instead, he is the most famous and richest investor in history. His superpowers were youth and compounding returns. We millennials need to follow his lead.

To build fortunes, we need to feel a greater sense of urgency. We need to be willing to take risks. Unfortunately, as I write, the millennial generation has not yet built up a large position in the stock market. In 2013, millennials owned just 6 percent of mutual funds assets in the United States; baby boomers owned 54 percent.[1] Boomers should own more because they are much further into their careers or retirement, but we millennials need to narrow this gap. Sadly, many of us are reluctant to invest because the financial crisis has crippled our willingness to take risks. Before the financial crisis, in 2008, we still had a healthy appetite for risk: 86 percent of millennials surveyed by the Investment Company Institute were willing to take an "average," "above-average," or "substantial" amount of risk; the remaining 14 percent surveyed were risk averse, saying they had a "below-average willingness" or "unwillingness" to take risk. But in 2009, after the market crash, the percentage of risk-averse millennials jumped from 14 percent to 20 percent and has risen since, to 25 percent in 2013.[2] Millennials in 2013 were even less willing to take risk than older people, aged 35 to 64. This is a travesty. We young people have the highest *ability* to take risk, but in 2014, we still don't have the proper *willingness* to do so. If we don't start investing when we're young, then we are squandering the best investing edge that we will ever have. We must remind ourselves that risk must be measured relative to our investment horizon; stocks are risky over the short term, but they are the least risky asset over the long term.

By going global, being different, and getting out of your own way, you'll avoid political and economic obstacles in the future and grow rich. This closing chapter summarizes the rules, tools, and services necessary to put your plan into action. It classifies your options as "good," "better," and "best" so that you can choose the most appropriate option for your particular circumstance. It also offers guidelines for building your own checklists, describes how to use the Millennial Money strategy, and suggests six books to read as you continue your market education.

Investing Hierarchy

There are many ways that investors can own stocks. They can buy individual stocks—as I suggest for the Millennial Money strategy—they can buy an index, or they can hire a professional who manages their portfolio in a mutual fund, an exchange traded fund (ETF), or a separate personalized account. These options all have their pros and cons, but before explaining each, we need a hierarchy for the best investment options. Figure 10.1 lists our options from good to best.

If you have a 401(k) or similar retirement account, your options may be limited. In this case, the best option is a global index fund, like one that mimics the MSCI All Country World Index ("good" option). Always choose a global option over a fund that just invests in your home country. If there are multiple options meeting this description, choose the one with the lowest fee. If there are "value"

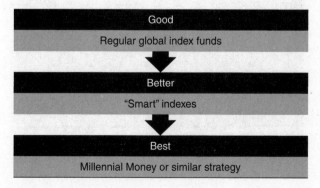

Figure 10.1   Hierarchy for Stock Market Investments

and "growth" options, choose value ("better" option). If there is no global option, a 50/50 split between a domestic index and an international index will suffice. Just remember to rebalance every year or two.

If you have an investment account with fewer constraints, then it is up to you whether you want to run a strategy like the Millennial Money strategy or hire someone else to run a strategy for you based on similar criteria. If you prefer that someone else manage your investments, then look for products like those described in chapter 5: indexes or strategies which are based on proven factors like value, quality, stakeholder yield, and momentum. These go by many different names: smart beta, equal-weighted indexes, fundamental indexes, value-weighted indexes, or alternative beta are all popular ways to describe a similar approach. If you hire a manager, then use the hierarchy in Figure 10.2.

Equal-weighted indexes are better than traditional, size-weighted indexes because they don't concentrate your portfolio in large-cap stocks. In an equal-weighted portfolio, Apple will no longer have a 4 percent weight; it will be more like 0.2 percent. Equal-weighted strategies have outperformed market-capitalization-weighted indexes over time.

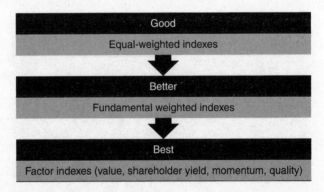

Figure 10.2   Hierarchy for Smart Strategies

Better still are fundamental indexes, which weight stocks according to their success as a business using attributes like cash flows, sales, and earnings. This method has grown very popular because it emphasizes stocks that are delivering the best results rather than stocks that are simply the biggest.

But the best option is a strategy that invests in stocks with the attributes from the Millennial Money checklist strategy. These include value (look for value-weighted indexes), stakeholder yield (also look for shareholder yield strategies), momentum (momentum-weighted strategies), and quality.

I believe that the Millennial Money strategy itself will deliver the strongest performance because it combines *all* these elements and builds concentrated portfolios—two features that are rare among other products run by professional money managers. There are also new strategies that invest in entire countries based on valuation and momentum—these are great options for building a global portfolio. Look for cyclically adjusted price-to-earnings (CAPE) based strategies. Small individual investors will always have an advantage because they can own very concentrated portfolios and don't have to worry about trading liquidity. You will earn the strongest returns if you build your own portfolios.

Smart strategies earned significant attention in 2014, and many analysts and journalists are describing them as marketing ploys that offer the same old market returns in shiny new packaging. These are false accusations, so long as the fees charged are not outrageous and the strategy itself is sound. Look for smart strategies that charge between 0.10 and 1 percent, and only pay 1 percent if the strategy is perfect: concentrated, different, and disciplined. There are many great options with a 0.50 to 0.75 percent fee, and even though smart strategies are more expensive than index funds, a better strategy justifies a higher fee. Smart strategies may also only invest in stocks in the United States or your home country, in which case they should be complemented by an international index fund (use the same hierarchy from Figure 10.1 to find the best available option).

No matter which option you choose, invest as much as you can. Remember that every dollar spent today could be worth anywhere from $15 to more than $90 in 40 years, depending on your rate of return.

Avoid Stock Picking

You'll notice that neither hierarchy, in Figure 10.1 or Figure 10.2, has a level for "pick stocks that you think will do well." Stock picking is difficult and time consuming. If you try to pick stocks, it will be hard to remain consistent, but easy to fall in love with an expensive stock. In 2013, my friends constantly asked me what I thought about Facebook, Twitter, Tesla, and Google—all very expensive at the time—but never asked me about companies like Seagate Technologies or Gap stores (two under-the-radar value stocks that did well). Stocks that capture our imaginations often crush our portfolios, but we will always be drawn to them like bugs to a flame. In 2014, I've been fielding questions about Uber and Snapchat while patiently buying boring, underpriced stocks that the market has neglected. Avoid picking stocks yourself—stick to a rules-based strategy instead.

A Word on Gold

I've also left out gold, which I get asked about all the time. Gold is an extremely tricky investment to evaluate. Unlike stocks—for which you can measure price against results like earnings, sales, and cash flow—gold has no "output" that we can use to evaluate its price. There's no price-to-earnings ratio for gold, there's just price. Gold also has a more limited history than stocks, because the price didn't change much between 1792 and 1971; the shorter time frame makes it harder to evaluate. People invest in gold mostly to protect themselves against the potential problems I discussed in the first two chapters: runaway inflation, currency devaluation, and even market crashes. Gold is insurance against the "world-is-going-to-hell" scenario.

But since 1971, gold has been a mediocre—but extremely volatile—investment. Since the Nixon Shock in August 1971, global stocks have delivered a much higher real annual return than gold (5.5 percent for stocks versus 3.8 percent for gold) and done so with 27 percent lower volatility (15.1 percent per year for stocks versus 20.6 percent for gold). The return of gold has also been very inconsistent across decades. It rose 26.4 percent per year (again, real) in the 1970s, then fell 7.6 percent per year in the '80s, fell 6.8 percent per year in the '90s, rose 14.2 percent between 2000 and 2011, and has fallen by 17 percent per year since, through December 2013.

After surging in the 1970s, gold hit a major peak in January 1980. But, as seen in Figure 10.3, after the 1980 peak, it crashed and has never recovered. Gold's price in dollars is higher today than it was in 1980, but adjusted for inflation it has gone nowhere. Despite its incredible run between 2000 and 2011, gold still sits 30 percent below its inflation-adjusted January 1980 peak. If you were a gold investor in 1980, you'd have nothing to show for it 34 years later. Stocks, in contrast, have never done so badly for so long. The average total real return for the global stock market across all 34-year periods was plus 662 percent and the *worst* return over a 34-year period was plus 406 percent.[3]

One criticism of this analysis is that the United States has not had the hyperinflation that gold is supposed to protect against, so

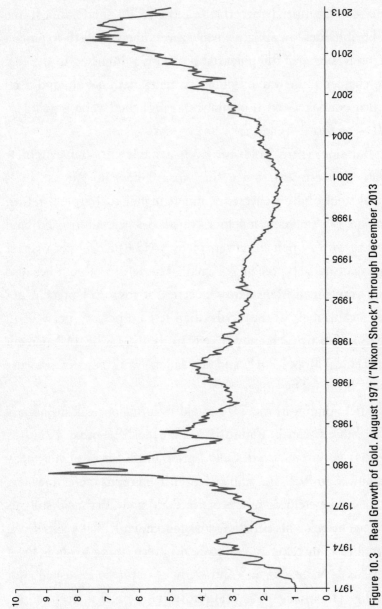

Figure 10.3   Real Growth of Gold. August 1971 ("Nixon Shock") through December 2013

Source: Monthly gold prices from Global Financial Data

even if gold hasn't been great since the 1970s, it might still offer valuable protection in the future. But gold hasn't always provided protection against hyperinflation. As authors Claude Erb and Campbell Harvey discuss in their paper "The Golden Dilemma," between 1980 and 2000, Brazilian inflation grew by 250 percent per year, but if you were a Brazilian citizen who invested in gold in 1980 and held it through 2000, your investment would still have declined by a real 70 percent—gold is supposed to protect your purchasing power, but it failed to do so in Brazil. Erb and Harvey say that one key finding from their exhaustive study is that "even though countries, such as the United States or Brazil, may experience very different inflation experiences...there is no reason to expect that the real gold return will be positive when a specific country experiences hyperinflation."[4]

Many famous and successful investors treat gold like a guilty pleasure, holding 5 percent of their portfolio in gold just in case. Feel free to do this if it helps you sleep better, but a global stock portfolio has offered better protection than gold for most of the things that might worry you. If you do buy gold, the GLD ETF is a fine option. To be extra careful (and maybe a little paranoid), buy physical gold bullion—bars and coins kept in a safe place. I've bought my wife a few pieces of gold jewelry, but that's about it. A "go bag" might be a better investment if you foresee a doomsday in the near future. I prefer my investments to produce tangible benefits in the form of dividends, cash flows, and share buybacks.

The Best Tools

If you choose to buy individual stocks with the Millennial Money checklist as your guide, here are several Web-based tools that I recommend for building your strategy and finding which stocks to buy each year:

- The American Association of Individual Investors (AAII, www.aaii.com) provides excellent resources for small investors at a very low annual fee: in 2013, an annual membership cost $29 and a lifetime member-ship cost $290. AAII's best feature is its stock screens—checklists from famous investors and the stocks that meet each checklist's criteria. You will be able to find the Millennial Money strategy on their website.

- Portfolio123 is more expensive—$29 a month—but also more flexible. Portfolio123 also has ready-made stock screens, but with its tool you can also build and test your own screens.

- Bloodhound Systems offers the most in-depth data and research of the three systems, but is also more expensive.

- The website turnkeyanalyst.com is run by Dr. Wesley Gray, author of the book *Quantitative Value*.[5] Gray's book suggests a strategy similar to the Millennial Money strategy, and his website provides information on his strategy and stocks currently meeting his criteria.

There are also several new companies that fully automate the entire investment process. None is perfect, but their auto-matic nature makes them very attractive options. Three com-panies have led the way: Personal Capital, Betterment, and Wealthfront. Each handles new investments, portfolio rebalanc-ing, and tax management. They are great "set-it-and-forget-it" options for the busy millennial investor. Personal Capital man-ages your money using strategies that are more similar to what I suggest in this book (they don't buy regular index funds), while

Betterment and Wealthfront opt for a pure index approach using ETFs.

Building Your Own Investment Checklist

Any of the tools above can help you develop your own strategy and style. If you do build your own strategy, stick to several key concepts and it will work well. Then, once the strategy is set, stay with it. Don't switch to a new one just because the original strategy hasn't worked for the last year or two. Follow these guidelines, which include what factors to look for (with the factors used in the Millennial Money strategy listed in italics).

Value over Growth.   Valuation should be the anchor for any strategy you choose. While growing sales, earnings, or market share may sound like great attributes to focus on, they do not matter as much as valuation. Always choose cheap stocks over expensive stocks. Factors to look for: *low enterprise value-to-free cash flow*, low price-to-cash flow, low price-to-earnings, low price-to-sales, low enterprise value-to-EBITDA (Earnings Before Interest, Taxes, Depreciation, and Amortization).

Quality over Junk.   Always favor high-quality companies over junk. Look for companies that earn high returns on their investments, have reasonable leverage, and have solid operating results led by strong cash flows. Fictitious earnings (weak cash flows) always spell trouble, and too much leverage can lead to disaster. Factors to look for: *high return on invested capital (ROIC)*, high return on assets (ROA), high return on equity (ROE), high interest coverage, *low accruals*.

Follow the Trend.   Market momentum over the past three to twelve months tends to persist into the future. Investing in companies with the *worst* momentum is like trying to catch a falling knife. No matter how cheap they may appear, they are often going to get even cheaper. Opt instead for stocks with strong recent price trends. Factors to look for: *high six-month momentum*, high nine-month momentum, low volatility.

Follow the Leaders.   Every CEO and CFO will be confident about their company's future, but we don't have the time or the reasons to listen to their words. We can, however, do well by following their actions. If they are sending cash back to stakeholders (through dividends, share repurchases, or debt pay down), then we should be interested. If they are raising cash from new stakeholders, run away. Factors to look for: *high stakeholder yield*, high shareholder yield, high dividend yield, high buybacks.

Running Your Strategy

The ideal holding period for any checklist stock (Millennial Money or other similar ranking or checklist strategy) is one year or longer. This will let the strategy work and keep you from trading too often. A one-year period also has distinct tax advantages in the United States. When it comes time to rebalance from last year's stocks to this year's, sell any stocks that you lost money on a few days before the one-year anniversary, to take advantage of short-term tax losses. Hold your winners a day or two longer than one year, so that any gains are taxed at the lower long-term capital gains tax rate.

To best match my results, you'll want to stagger your investments throughout the year. If you have $10,000 to invest, for example, use $5,000, $3,333, or $2,500 to invest in the best ten to twenty names on day one. Then invest the next chunk in ten to twenty more stocks in month 6 ($5000), months 4 and 8 ($3,333), or months 3, 6, and 9 ($2,500). You'll achieve the smoothest results if you invest in four different quarterly buckets ($2,500 increments), but all methods will work. You can think of the quarterly option ($2,500) as maintaining four separate portfolios, all of which are rebalanced once per year. This is the best method because you will spread your bets a little more and be able to take advantage of new opportunities as they present themselves throughout the year, rather than just once per year. Regardless of what frequency you choose, sell stocks that no longer meet the checklist at rebalance time, and use the sales proceeds to buy new stocks that do. If a stock still meets the criteria, just hold on to it.

If you opt instead for a portfolio of smart ETFs or mutual funds, choose your allocation and stick to it. One of the easiest methods would be to choose a global, value-based ETF. I am partial to my friend Mebane Faber's Shareholder Yield and Global Value ETFs. His company, Cambria Investment Management, offers both international and US versions of the shareholder-yield ETF, which both incorporate shareholder yield and other elements like value and momentum. Cambria's global-value strategy buys stocks in the cheapest markets around the globe. Cambria's ETFs are also very concentrated, similar to the Millennial Money strategy; each holds 100 stocks. Other firms that manage fantastic ETFs, mutual funds, and separate account strategies that line up with my suggestion to "be different" are Dimensional Fund Advisors (aka DFA), O'Shaughnessy Asset Management (my firm), Wisdom Tree, and Research Affiliates. If you choose multiple smart ETFs or mutual funds, rebalance them back to target weights every year or two.

What to Read Next

When I graduated from college, I had never built a spreadsheet and didn't know the first thing about markets. My personal investing journey started with a plunge into books. To understand the market, there is no substitute for reading. Here are six of my favorite books about the market and investor behavior.

- *What Works on Wall Street* by James O'Shaughnessy: A pioneering work on stock selection strategies, now in its fourth edition. I didn't read my dad's book until I was 20 (whoops) but when I did, it ignited my interest in the stock market. I've been incredibly lucky to have him as my inspiration and mentor. I was also a contributing author to the fourth edition, which inspired me to write *Millennial Money.*

- *Inside the Investor's Brain* by Richard Peterson: My favorite book on investor behavior. Peterson covers every aspect of the investor's psyche, and offers strategies for overcoming our inherent faults. If you want to ensure you get and *stay* out of your own way, read this book.

- *Reminiscences of a Stock Operator* by Edwin Lefèvre: An all-time classic written from the perspective of Jesse Livermore. As Livermore explains in the book, "Nowhere does history indulge in repetitions so often or so uniformly as in Wall Street. When you read contemporary accounts of booms or panics the one thing that strikes you most forcibly is how little either stock speculation or stock speculators today differ from yesterday. The game does not change and neither does human nature."

- *The (mis)Behavior of Markets* by Benoît B. Mandelbrot: The famous mathematician turns his sights on the stock market and debunks the idea that markets are efficient.

- *Devil Take the Hindmost: A History of Financial Speculation* by Edward Chancellor: Chancellor is a great writer and his entire book is filled with cautionary tales: stranger-than-fiction stories about market speculators, bubbles, and crashes.

- *Contrarian Investment Strategies: The Psychological Edge* by David Dreman: Dreman has had a long and successful career writing and managing money using a contrarian, value-based investing strategy. Dreman explains how and why value investing works in entertaining fashion.

Millennial Money

In India, two animals represent two ways of looking at the world: the way of the monkey and the way of the kitten.[6] A kitten meows and his mother picks him up by the neck and delivers him to safety. Kittens are well taken care of. Baby monkeys don't have that luxury. When a baby's mother is moving, the baby holds onto her back for dear life. Baby monkeys have to take care of themselves— they have to find their own way. We need to be monkeys. We may be able to rely on our governments and others to support us later in life, but probably not to the extent that current retirees do. If your company offers a 401(k), begin or increase your allocation. Open up an investment account at Personal Capital, Betterment, Wealthfront, Charles Schwab, or Fidelity. Set up automatic contributions to these accounts directly from your paycheck or from your checking account.

We millennials face unique and significant obstacles, but we also have unique advantages. We will have to support the retiring and aging baby boom generation, but luckily our generation matches theirs in size. We've witnessed two market disasters early in our lives and are therefore skeptical of the stock market. But our skepticism is misplaced, because for more than 100 years there has been no safer place for money than the global stock market.

Student loans and a difficult job market are real and significant impediments to making our first investments in the global stock market, but there will always be reasons *not* to invest. Living in the information age is a gift and a curse. Technology has made owning stocks easy and cheap, so stock ownership should become more and more universal. People at all income levels can participate in the growth of the global stock market. But more technology means more information and more noise. For any stock, strategy, or index you own, there will be constant news that may compel you to sell in panic. And when you are losing to the market, there will be bubbles, large and small, luring you away from your laggard portfolio. The correct decision will be to do nothing, or, if you have the intestinal fortitude, buy more when others are selling. The combination of youth and easy access to great investment strategies is our edge, and the reasons *to* invest outweigh every reason not to invest.

The market is a competitive place. The victors live off the losses of the losers. Losers move in and out of the market according to their emotional reactions, they buy exciting and expensive stocks, change strategies when times get tough, and trade too often. Winners focus on the long term, remain patient, do not attempt to time the market, buy unloved but solid companies, and do not react to noise in the news. One sneaky way to succeed is to refuse to fight: just buy low-fee index funds that will grow at a nice pace over time. This is a fine option, so long as you stay put in the market. But superior returns are possible. Using the principles laid out in this book for buying stocks, you can build a strategy that outpaces index funds and compounds your young money into an impressive fortune. Fortunes start small. You have the acorns that can become mighty oaks. You just need to plant them.

NOTES

Introduction

1. Survey conducted by Harris Interactive on behalf of Think Finance, April 25–May 7, 2013, available at http://www.harrisinteractive.com/vault /Harris-ThinkFinance-Survey-Release6-11-13.pdf.
2. Survey conducted by Wells Fargo, May 22, 2013, available at https://www .wellsfargo.com/press/2013/20130522_MorethanhalfofMillennials.

1 The Millennial Edge

1. "Think You Know the Next Gen Investor? Think Again," UBS Investor Watch: Analyzing Investor Sentiment and Behavior, 1Q 2014, available at http:// www.static-ubs.com/us/en/wealth/misc/investor-watch/_jcr _content/par/columncontrol_0/col2/textimage.1213349454.file/dGV4d D0vY29udGVudC9kYW0vV2VhbHRoTWFuYWdlbWVudEFt ZXJpY2FzL2RvY3VtZW50cy9pbnZlc3Rvci13YXRjaC0xUTI wMTQtcmVwb3b3 J0LnBkZg==/investor-watch-1Q2014-report.pdf.
2. Ibid.
3. Ibid.
4. Assuming that the $10,000 annual contribution grows with inflation of 4 percent per year.
5. Glyn Davies, *A History of Money: From Ancient Times to the Present Day*, 2nd ed. (Cardiff: University of Wales Press, 2002).
6. Money is defined as M2: a measure of money supply that includes cash, checking deposits, savings deposits, money market mutual funds, and other time deposits, which can be quickly converted into cash; data from the World Gold Council, St. Louis Federal Reserve; author's calculations.
7. Jack Weatherford, *The History of Money* (New York: Three Rivers Press, 1997).
8. 30-day T-bills are used as proxy for savings account rate of return.

9. Data from Roger Ibbotson; author's calculations. Data series for T-bills, stocks, and inflation begin January 1926.

10. Annual data from Elroy Dimson, Paul Marsh, and Mike Staunton; author's calculations.

11. Stock market referenced is the S&P 500.

2   Building Good Financial Karma

1. Assumes that the $17,500 contribution limit grows with inflation. Inflation assumption is post-1971 inflation of 4.23 percent per year.

2. Data from Emmanuel Saez, available at http://emlab.berkeley.edu/users /saez under "Income and Wealth Inequality."

3. Jonathan V. Last, *What to Expect When No One's Expecting: America's Coming Demographic Disaster*, 1st ed. (New York: Encounter Books, 2013).

4. Ibid.

5. As of 2011, data from the World Bank, available at http://data.worldbank .org/indicator/SP.DYN.TFRT.IN.

6. Last, *What to Expect When No One's Expecting.*

7. Sonia Arrison, *100 Plus: How the Coming Age of Longevity Will Change Everything, from Careers and Relationships to Family and Faith* (New York: Basic Books, 2011).

8. Laurence J. Kotlikoff and Scott Burns, *The Coming Generational Storm: What You Need to Know about America's Economic Future* (Cambridge, MA: MIT Press, 2005).

9. Last, *What to Expect When No One's Expecting.*

10. Assumes 80 million millennials against a population of 313 million Americans, as of July 2013.

11. Data from United Nations, available at http://esa.un.org/unpd/wpp /Excel-Data/population.htm, table "Old-Age Dependency Ratio 2"; author's calculations for number of workers to cover those aged 65+.

12. 2030 is the year that the first millennials will reach age 50, and 2050 is when the tail end of the millennial generation will reach age 50.

13. Ted C. Fishman, *Shock of Gray: The Aging of the World's Population and How It Pits Young against Old, Child against Parent, Worker against Boss, Company against Rival, and Nation against Nation* (New York: Scribner, 2010).

14. Data from the White House, available at http://www.whitehouse.gov/omb /budget/historicals, Table 3.1.

15. As calculated by Professor Laurence Kotlikoff, Boston University.

16. Data from Congressional Budget Office, available at http://www.cbo.gov/sites /default/files/cbofiles/attachments/06-05-Long-Term_Budget_Outlook_2. pdf.

17. Data from the White House, available: http://www.whitehouse.gov/omb /budget/historicals, Table 3.1. This does not include the first year over year increase (24-fold increase) between 1966 and 1987.

18. By 2040.

19. 2013 Annual Report of the Boards of Trustees of the Federal Hospital Insurance and Federal Supplementary Medical Insurance Trust Funds, available at http://www.cms.gov/Research-Statistics-Data-and-Systems/Statistics -Trends-and-Reports/ReportsTrustFunds/Downloads/TR2013.pdf.

20. Ibid.

21. Data from Congressional Budget Office, available at http://www.cbo .gov/sites/default/files/cbofiles/attachments/06-05-Long-Term_Budget _Outlook_2.pdf.

22. To be fair, we could raise the retirement age from 65, which would effectively reduce the number of old people as far as our government is concerned.

23. Forty-five countries in the MSCI All Country World Stock Index.

24. Data from the World Bank, available at http://databank.worldbank.org/data /views/variableselection/selectvariables.aspx?source=worldwide-governance -indicators.

4 Go Global

1. Edward Chancellor, *Devil Take the Hindmost: A History of Financial Speculation* (New York: Plume, 2000).

2. Ibid.

3. Total return between January 1990 and June 2013.

4. MSCI All Country World Index, January 1990 to June 2013.

5. B. Mark Smith, *A History of the Global Stock Market from Ancient Rome to Silicon Valley,* 1st ed. (Chicago: University of Chicago Press, 2004).

6. Ibid.

7. Data from Elroy Dimson, Paul Marsh, and Mike Staunton; author's calculations.

8. Mary Buffett and David Clark, *The Tao of Warren Buffett: Warren Buffett's Words of Wisdom: Quotations and Interpretations to Help Guide You to Billionaire Wealth and Enlightened Business Management* (New York: Scribner, 2006).

9. Christopher B. Philips, Francis M. Kinniry Jr., and Scott J. Donaldson, "The Role of Home Bias in Global Asset Allocation Decisions," *Vanguard Research*, June 2012, available at https://advisors.vanguard.com/iwe/pdf/ICRRHB.pdf.

10. "2013 Global R&D Funding Forecast," sponsored by Battelle and *R&D Mag*, available at http://www.rdmag.com/sites/rdmag.com/files/GFF2013 Final2013_reduced.pdf.

11. The exact return would be 15.5 percent: $10\% + 5\% + (10\% \times 5\%) = 15.5\%$.

12. Based on monthly returns for the MSCI World Index in local and US dollar terms, January 1970 to June 2013.

13. All American depository receipts (ADRs) or other foreign stocks listed on a US stock exchange with a market capitalization of at least $50 million.

5   Be Different

1. O'Shaughnessy Asset Management's Market Leaders Value Composite Returns, November 2007 to February 2009.

2. O'Shaughnessy Asset Management's Market Leaders Value Composite Returns versus the S&P 500.

3. Miller stopped managing the Legg Mason Value Trust in 2011, but continued to manage the Opportunity Fund through 2013. Fund return data from Morningstar.com.

4. The Dow Jones Industrial Average is a notable exception to this rule, because each company's weight is determined by its stock price rather than its market capitalization.

5. All US and world equity mutual funds; data from Investment Company Institute and The Leuthold Group.

6. "Think You Know the Next Gen Investor? Think Again," UBS Investor Watch: Analyzing Investor Sentiment and Behavior, firstquarter 2014, available at http://www.static-ubs.com/us/en/wealth/misc/investor -watch/_jcr_content/par/columncontrol_0/col2/textimage.1213349454 .file/dGV4dD0vY29udGVudC9kYW0vV2VhbHRoTWFuYWdlbW VudEFtZXJpY2FzL2RvY3VtZW50cy9pbnZlc3Rvci13YXRjaC0xUTI wMTQtcmVwb3J0LnBkZg==/investor-watch-1Q2014-report.pdf.

7. James O'Shaughnessy, *What Works on Wall Street: The Classic Guide to the Best-Performing Investment Strategies of All Time*, 4th ed. (New York: McGraw-Hill, 2012)

8. S&P Indexes versus Active Funds (SPIVA) Scorecard, 2012, from S&P Dow Jones Indexes, available at http://www.spindexes.com/resource-center /thought-leadership/spiva/.

9. Ibid.

10. Fama does, however, believe that certain "risk factors" like valuation and market capitalization (small being better) can lead to market beating returns.

11. This strategy buys all companies that begin with the letter C and weights them equally in the portfolio. The portfolio is rebalanced annually.

12. To measure cheapness for the Sector Bargains strategy, I combine several simple valuation measures: price-to-sales, price-to-earnings, price-to-operating cash flow, earnings before interest, taxes and depreciation to total enterprise value, dividend yield, and share repurchase yield. These five factors are equally weighted to determine an overall value "score."

13. January 1979 to July 2013. These returns are so impressive because Russell's Value indexes still use market capitalization to weight stocks in the index once the cheaper stocks have been selected. Value indexes that *don't* use market capitalization to weight stocks should perform even better.

14. To determine average 30-year excess return, I calculate the annual geometric mean of the strategy and the S&P 500 and compound that return over 30 years. I then take a simple difference between the two results.

15. To eliminate the problem of seasonality, the strategies are run with starting dates in each of the twelve months of the year and the twelve separate results are averaged. This approach would be similar to opening an account during each month of the year and rebalancing each account once per year.

16. To measure momentum, I use 3-month, 6-month, and 9-month total return, and 12-month return volatility. These four factors are equally weighted to determine an overall momentum "score."

17. Shareholder yield is calculated as current dividend yield plus the percentage of shares outstanding repurchased or issued over the prior twelve-month period.

18. Volatility is calculated as the standard deviation of the last twelve monthly total returns.

19. Earnings quality is defined as (net income − operating cash flow) / market capitalization.

20. M. Cremers and A. Petajisto, "How Active Is Your Manager? A New Metric that Predicts Performance," March 31, 2009, available at http://www .iaclarington.com/docs/email/2012/05/HowActiveIsYourManager.pdf.

6 The Millennial Money Strategy

1. Daniel Kahneman, *Thinking: Fast and Slow*, 1st ed. (New York: Farrar, Straus and Giroux, 2011).

2. Atul Gawande, *The Checklist Manifesto: How to Get Things Right*, 1st ed. (New York: Metropolitan Books, 2010).

3. I have modified this from his original checklist slightly to make it simpler and clearer. For the full checklist, see chapter 14 of Ben Graham's *The Intelligent Investor*, 4th ed. rev. (New York: Harper Business, 1973).

4. David J. Leinweber, "Stupid Data Miner Tricks: Over Fitting the S&P 500," 1995, available at http://nerdsonwallstreet.typepad.com/my_weblog/files /dataminejune_2000.pdf.

5. Value score 1–100 based on price-to-sales, price-to-earnings, EBITDA-to-enterprise value, free cash flow-to-enterprise value, dividend yield, and share buybacks.

6. January 31, 1963 to June 30, 2013; Capex growth calculated as year-over-year percentage change using raw data from S&P Compustat.

7. September 30, 1989 to June 30, 2013; Goodwill growth calculated as year-over-year percentage change using raw data from S&P Compustat.

8. December 31, 1972 to June 30, 2013; financing cash flows calculated using raw data from S&P Compustat.

9. Ken Favaro, Per-Ola Karlsson, and Gary Neilson, "CEO Succession 2000–2009: A Decade of Convergence and Compression," Strategy+Business, 2010, available at http://www.booz.com/global/home/what-we-think/reports-white -papers/article-display/succession-2000–2009-decade-convergence.

10. December 31, 1972 to June 30, 2013; financing cash flows calculated using raw data from S&P Compustat.

11. Return on invested capital defined as operating income divided by invested capital (book value of equity + book value of debt – cash).

12. Alfred Rappaport, *Creating Shareholder Value: A Guide For Managers And Investors*, rev. (New York: The Free Press, 1998).

13. John Graham, Campbell Harvey, and Shiva Rajgopal, "The Economic Implications of Corporate Financial Reporting," Working Paper no. 10550, National Bureau of Economic Research, June 2004.

14. Ibid.

15. "Biography: Sir John Templeton," http://www.sirjohntempleton.org/biography .asp.

16. High-yielding stock is defined as the 20 percent of dividend-paying companies with the highest dividend yields at any given time.

17. Enterprise value, similar to takeover value of the company = market value of equity + book value of debt – cash.

18. The high-momentum portfolio (best decile by six-month total return) has an annual volatility of 22.8 percent versus 15 percent for the S&P 500 during the same period (1963–2013).

19. John C. Bogle, *Don't Count on It!: Reflections on Investment Illusions, Capitalism, "Mutual" Funds, Indexing, Entrepreneurship, Idealism, and Heroes* (Hoboken, NJ: John Wiley, 2011).

7   Get Out of Your Own Way

1. Nancy Segal, *Entwined Lives: Twins and What They Tell Us about Human Behavior* (New York: Plume, 2000).

2. Thomas J. Bouchard Jr., David T. Lykken, Matthew McGue, Nancy L. Segal, and Auke Tellegen, "Sources of Human Psychological Differences: The Minnesota Study of Twins Reared Apart," *Science* 250, no. 4978 (1990): 223–228.

3. Lawrence Wright, *Twins: And What They Tell Us about Who We Are* (New York: John Wiley, 1997).

4. Segal, *Entwined Lives.*

5. Ibid.

6. Henrik Cronqvist and Stephan Siegel, "Why Do Individuals Exhibit Investment Biases?," 2012, available at http://www2.warwick.ac.uk/fac/soc/wbs/subjects/finance/seminars/investment_biases.pdf.

7. Philip Zimbardo and John Boyd, *The Time Paradox: The New Psychology of Time that Will Change Your Life* (New York: Free Press, 2008).

8. Twenty years ending June 30, 2013.

9. John C. Bogle, *Don't Count on It!: Reflections on Investment Illusions, Capitalism, "Mutual" Funds, Indexing, Entrepreneurship, Idealism, and Heroes* (Hoboken, NJ: John Wiley, 2011).

10. Data from Morningstar, Oceanstone Fund (OSFDX) as of October 31, 2013; investor return (behavior-adjusted) vs. total return (buy-and-hold).

11. Through September 30, 2013.

12. Data from Morningstar, Vanguard 500 Index Inv (VFINX) as of October 31, 2013; investor return (behavior-adjusted) vs. total return (buy-and-hold).

13. David DiSalvo, *What Makes Your Brain Happy and Why You Should Do the Opposite* (Amherst, NY: Prometheus Books, 2011).

14. Michael Gazzaniga, *Who's in Charge?: Free Will and the Science of the Brain* (New York: Ecco, 2012).

15. Adam Alter, *Drunk Tank Pink: And Other Unexpected Forces that Shape How We Think, Feel, and Behave* (New York: Penguin Press, 2012).

16. Kerri Smith, "Neuroscience vs. Philosophy: Taking Aim at Free Will," *Nature*, August 31, 2011, available at http://www.nature.com/news/2011/110831/full/477023a.html.

17. Alter, *Drunk Tank Pink*.

18. David Hirshleifer and Tyler Shumway, "Good Day Sunshine: Stock Returns and Weather," 2001, available at http://www-personal.umich.edu/~shumway/papers.dir/weather.pdf.

19. Ulrike Malmendier and Stefan Nagel, "Depression Babies: Do Macro-economic Experiences Affect Risk Taking?" NBER working paper no. 14813, 2009, available at http://www.nber.org/papers/w14813.

20. Brad M. Barber and Terrance Odean, "All That Glitters: The Effect of Attention and News on the Buying Behavior of Individual and Institutional Investors," 2007, available at http://faculty.haas.berkeley.edu/odean/Papers%20current%20versions/AllThatGlitters_RFS_2008.pdf.

21. Brad M. Barber and Terrance Odean, "Boys Will Be Boys: Gender, Overconfidence, and Common Stock Investment," 2001, available at http://faculty.haas.berkeley.edu/odean/papers/gender/BoysWillBeBoys.pdf.

22. Ibid.

23. Ibid.

24. Alter, *Drunk Tank Pink*.

25. Richard Thaler, "Opting in vs. Opting Out," *New York Times*, September 26, 2009, http://www.nytimes.com/2009/09/27/business/economy/27view.html.

26. Ibid.

27. C. Madrian and Dennis F. Shea, "The Power of Suggestion: Inertia in 401(k) Participation and Savings Behavior," *Quarterly Journal of Economics* 116, no. 4 (November 2001): 1149–1187.

28. Ibid.

8   The Long Game

1. http://www.10000yearclock.net/learnmore.html.

2. Ibid.

3. Walter Mischel, Yuichi Shoda, and Monica L. Rodriguez, "Delay of Gratification in Children," *Science* 244 (1989): 933–938; Ozlem N. Ayduk, Rodolfo Mendoa-Denton, Walter Mischel, Geraldine Downey, Philip K. Peake, and Monica L. Rodriguez, "Regulating the Interpersonal Self: Strategic

Self-Regulation for Coping with Rejection Sensitivity," *Journal of Personality and Social Psychology* 79 (2000): 776–792; Tanya R. Schlam, Nicole L. Wilson, Yuichi Shoda, Walter Mischel, and Ozlem Ayduk, "Preschoolers' Delay of Gratification Predicts Their Body Mass 30 Years Later," *Journal of Pediatrics* 162 (January 2013): 90–93.

4. Shane Frederick, George Lowenstein, and Ted O'Donoghue, "Time Discounting and Time Preference: A Critical Review," *Journal of Economic Literature* 40 (2002): 351–401.

5. Richard H. Thaler, "Some Empirical Evidence on Dynamic Inconsistency," *Economic Letters* 8, no. 3 (1981): 201–207.

6. Samuel M. McClure, David I. Laibson, George Loewenstein, and Jonathan D. Cohen, "Separate Neural Systems Value Immediate and Delayed Monetary Rewards," *Science* 306, no. 5695 (October 15, 2004): 503–507.

7. Susan Hagen, "The Marshmallow Study Revisited," available at http://www.rochester.edu/news/show.php?id=4622.

8. Data on S&P 500 (stocks), long-term government bonds (bonds), and T-bills (cash) from Roger Ibbotson, 1926–2013.

9. Paul B. Andreassen, "Judgmental Extrapolation and Market Overreaction: On the Use and Disuse of News," *Journal of Behavioral Decision Making* 3 (1990): 153–174.

10. Returns for March 2009 to September 2013.

11. Jason Zweig, *Your Money & Your Brain: How the New Science of Neuroeconomics Can Help Make You Rich* (New York: Simon and Schuster, 2007).

12. Ivo Welch, "Views of Financial Economists on the Equity Premium and on Professional Controversies," *Journal of Business* 73, no. 4 (October 2000): 501–537.

13. Ivo Welch, "The Equity Premium Consensus Forecast Revisited," Cowles Foundation discussion paper no. 1325, September, 2001.

14. J. Madeline Nash, "Addicted," *Time*, May 5, 1997.

15. Hannah M. Bayer and Paul W. Glimcher, "Midbrain Dopamine Neurons Encode a Quantitative Reward Prediction Error Signal," *Neuron*, 47, no. 1 (2005): 129–141.

16. Martijn Cremers, Miguel Ferreira, Pedro Matos, and Laura Starks, "The Mutual Fund Industry Worldwide: Explicit and Closet Indexing, Fees, and Performance," September 2013, available at http://papers.ssrn.com/sol3/papers.cfm?abstract_id=1830207.

17. Ibid.

18. Amit Goyal and Sunil Wahal, "The Selection and Termination of Investment Management Firms by Plan Sponsors," *Journal of Finance* 63, no. 4 (August 2008): 1805–1847.

9 The Push and the Pull

1. Jared Diamond, *The World until Yesterday: What Can We Learn from Traditional Societies?* (New York: Viking, 2012).

2. Ibid.

3. Daniel Kahneman and Amos Tversky, "Prospect Theory: An Analysis of Decision under Risk," *Econometrica*, 47, no. 2 (March 1979): 263–291.

4. E. Yang, D. H. Zald, and R. Blake, "Fearful Expressions Gain Preferential Access to Awareness during Continuous Flash Suppression," *Emotion* 7, no. 4 (2007): 882–886.

5. Mark A. Williams, Adam P. Morris, Francis McGlone, David F. Abbott, and Jason B. Mattingley, "Amygdala Responses to Fearful and Happy Facial Expressions under Conditions of Binocular Suppression," *Journal of Neuroscience* 24, no. 12 (2004): 2898–2904.

6. R. F. Baumeister, E. Bratslavsky, C. Finkenauer, and K. D. Vohs, "Bad Is Stronger than Good," *Review of General Psychology* 5 (2001): 323–370.

7. Daniel Kahneman, *Thinking, Fast and Slow,* 1st ed. (New York: Farrar, Straus and Giroux, 2011).

8. Rick Hanson, *Buddha's Brain: The Practical Neuroscience of Happiness, Love, and Wisdom* (Oakland, CA: New Harbinger, 2009).

9. "Lessons from the Brain-Damaged Investor" by Jane Spencer, *The Wall Street Journal*, July 21, 2005, available at http://online.wsj.com/news/articles/SB112190164023291519.

10. S&P 500 and long-term US government bonds.

11. Robert M. Sapolsky, *Monkeyluv: And Other Essays on Our Lives as Animals* (New York: Scribner, 2005).

12. Richard L. Peterson, *Inside the Investor's Brain: The Power of Mind over Money* (Hoboken, NJ: John Wiley, 2007).

13. Daniel Gilbert, "What You Don't Know Makes You Nervous," *New York Times*, May 21, 2009, available at http://query.nytimes.com/gst/fullpage.html?res=9A0DEFD71630F932A15756C0A96F9C8B63.

14. Sapolsky, *Monkeyluv.*

15. S&P 500 data, with extension, from Global Financial Data; ten-year P/E data from Robert Schiller.

16. Mebane Faber, Cambria Investment Management, available at http://online.wsj.com/news/interactive/BUBBLE20131116?ref=SB10001424052702303559504579197830356373734.

17. Hans C. Breiter, Itzhak Aharon, Daniel Kahneman, Anders Dale, and Peter Shizgal, "Functional Imaging of Neural Responses to Expectancy and Experience of Monetary Gains and Losses," *Neuron* 30 (May 2001): 619–639.

18. Wolfram Schultz, Paul Apicella, and Tomas Ljungberg, "Responses of Monkey Dopamine Neurons to Reward and Conditioned Stimuli during Successive Steps of Learning a Delayed Response Task," *Journal of Neuroscience* 13, no. 3 (1993): 900–913.

19. Sapolsky, *Monkeyluv.*

20. Daniel Kahneman, *Thinking, Fast and Slow,* 1st ed (New York: Farrar, Straus and Giroux, 2011).

21. Based on daily prices collected from John Castaing.

22. Joseph Campbell, *A Hero with a Thousand Faces* (Novato, CA: New World Library, 2008).

10   Opportunity Knocks

1. "Ownership of Mutual Funds, Shareholder Sentiment, and Use of the Internet, 2013," available at http://www.ici.org/pdf/per19–09.pdf.

2. Ibid.

3. MSCI World returns in US dollars, 1971–2013.

4. Claude B. Erb and Campbell R. Harvey, "The Golden Dilemma," available at http://papers.ssrn.com/sol3/papers.cfm?abstract_id=2078535.

5. Wesley R. Gray, PhD, and Tobias E. Carlisle, *Quantitative Value: A Practitioner's Guide to Automating Intelligent Investment and Eliminating Behavioral Errors* (Hoboken, NJ: Wiley Finance, 2013).

6. Joseph Campbell, *Myths to Live By (The Collected Works of Joseph Campbell)* (Stillpoint Digital Press, 2011).

INDEX

401(k), 33, 140–1, 184, 195. *See also* retirement plans

active share, 86–8, 119
aging population, 3, 37–9, 42, 45–7, 59, 195. *See also* baby boom generation
allocation, portfolio, 14, 61–2, 132–3, 140, 193, 195
alternative (smart) indexes, 71, 80–3, 85, 88–9, 91, 116, 123, 141, 183, 193. *See also* smart strategies
Amazon.com, 78, 143–4
American Association of Individual Investors (AAII), 120–1, 132–4, 190
Andreassen, Paul, 153
Apple, 3, 50, 55, 63, 72–3, 78–9, 136, 139, 178, 184
Asimov, Isaac, 89, 154
AstraZeneca, 66
AT&T, 78
Australia, 26–7
Austria, 26–7, 60, 139

baby boom generation, 14, 37–8, 42–3, 46, 50, 58, 74, 110, 182, 195
Barber, Brad, 137–8
Beane, Billy, 80
bear markets, 130, 133, 148, 151, 167, 172–3
behavior-adjusted return, 129–30, 132–3
Belgium, 26–7, 60
Bernanke, Ben, 22
Betterment, 190–1, 195
Bezos, Jeff, 144
Bitcoin, 176–7, 179
Bloodhound System, 121, 190
Bogle, John, 123
bonds, 3, 26–7, 110, 132–3, 140, 149–51, 156, 168–71
Botswana, 108–9, 163–5
Brazil, 173, 189
Bretton Woods Agreement, 20

bubbles, market, 29, 59, 129–30, 133, 156, 173, 175–9
Buffett, Warren, 61, 76, 102, 111, 181
bull markets, 58, 133, 148, 156, 170, 172, 179
buy-and-hold return, 129–30, 132, 141

Cambria Investment Management, 193
Campbell, Joseph, 7, 171, 179
Canada, 26–7, 54, 158–9
career risk, 157–9
cash allocation, 3, 14, 18, 22–6, 132–3, 140, 149, 151, 153
cash fiends, 100–1
cash flow, 84–5, 98, 102–6, 111–12, 116–19, 121, 191
cause and effect (karma), 31–4, 40, 42, 48, 51
central banks, 22
Chancellor, Edward, 194–5
Charles Schwab, 65, 141, 195
Checklist Manifesto, The (Gawande), 94–5, 116
checklists, 94–8, 116, 118–24, 189–93. *See also* Millennial Money strategy: and checklist approach
China, 42, 63
Cisco, 79
Civil War, American, 20–1
Clinton, Bill, 34–5
closet indexing, 158–60
Coca-Cola, 5, 62, 103
Coinage Act of 1792, 19–20
Columbus, Christopher, 8
compounding, 7, 28–9, 34
  and cheap stock, 81
  and delayed gratification, 144, 148
  and fees, 123
  explained, 15–19
  and return on investment, 104
  and Sector Leaders strategy, 78

compounding costs, tyranny of, 123
Congressional Budget Office (CBO), 43, 46–7
consistency, 91–5
Contrarian Investment Strategies: The Psychological Edge (Dreman), 195
Cremers, Martijn, 86–7
Crichton, Michael, 57–8
Cronqvist, Henrik, 127
cyclically adjusted price-to-earnings (CAPE), 185

debt
    company, 96, 98, 101–2, 116, 192
    and karma, 42–5, 47–8, 59, 63
    national, 42–5, 47–8
    responsible, 43–4
    student loans, 13, 33, 196
default options, 139–40
delayed gratification, 144–8
demographics, 35–7, 49
Denmark, 26–7
devaluation, currency, 18, 53, 187
Devil Take the Hindmost: A History of Financial Speculation (Chancellor), 194–5
Diamond, Jared, 164
Dimensional Fund Advisors (DFA), 193
Dimson, Elroy, 66
DiSalvo, David, 134
dopamine, 156–7, 174
Dow Jones Industrial Average (DJIA), 49–50, 72
Dreman, David, 195
Duke Energy Corporation, 78
Dumb and Dumber (film), 47–8

earnings, 98, 101, 103–8, 110–12, 117–18, 172–3, 178. *See also* price-to-earnings ratio
Edison, Thomas, 49
Emerson, Ralph Waldo, 153
empire builders, 99–100, 112
enterprise value-to-EBITDA, 191
enterprise-value-to-free cash flow, 112, 117–18, 191
equal-weighted indexes, 184
Erb, Claude, 189
exchange traded funds (ETFs), 28, 60, 66–7, 71, 183
ExxonMobil, 55, 78–9

Faber, Mebane, 193
Fama, Eugene, 76
fear, 5, 56, 93, 109–11, 142, 161, 165–74, 179–80

Federal Insurance Contributions Act (FICA), 44, 48
fees, 74–6, 121–3, 158–60, 185–6
fertility rates, 36–7
fiat money system, 19–20, 22, 24, 27, 59
Fidelity, 195
financial crisis of 2008, 62, 69–70, 148, 153–4, 169, 171, 182
financial karma, 31–4, 40, 42, 48, 51
Finland, 26–7
FinViz, 121
fiscal gap, 42
foreign investments. *See* global investments
France, 26–7, 60, 159, 172
free cash flow, 112, 117–18, 121, 191
fundamental indexes, 184–5

Gawande, Atul, 94–5, 116
Gazzaniga, Michael, 134–5
General Electric (GE), 49–50, 54, 78–9, 136
Generation X, 14
Germany, 59–60, 139, 26–7
Gladwell, Malcolm, 135
Global Innovation Rankings, 62–3
global investments, 3, 5–9, 28, 47, 55, 57–67, 177, 185, 189, 193, 195–6
    and index funds, 59–60, 72, 183, 186
    and P/E ratios, 172–3
    and risk, 54, 61, 65–7
    and Sector Bargains strategy, 82–3
gold, 18–22, 176–7, 186–9
Goodman, George, 22
Google, 50, 117, 178, 186
Goyal, Amit, 159–60
Graham, Benjamin, 95–7, 102, 151
Gray, Wesley, 190
Great Depression, 20–1, 24, 149–51
Greece, 47, 173
greed, 5, 56, 142, 161, 165, 172–80
Greenblatt, Joel, 116
gross domestic product (GDP), 40, 43, 47, 73
Gulliver's Travels (Swift), 45–6

Hanson, Rick, 167
Harvey, Campbell, 189
heroes as risk-takers, 7–8
hyperinflation, 60, 187–9. *See also* inflation

income inequality, 34–5, 42
index funds, 28, 55–6, 196
    arguments for, 73–6
    and closet indexing, 158–9
    explained, 73
    and fees, 74–5, 122–3
    global, 59–60, 72, 183, 186

index funds—*Continued*
and Sector Leaders strategy, 77–9
smart, 71, 80–3, 85, 88–9, 91, 116, 123,
141, 183, 193
as a starting point, 89
Vanguard S&P 500 index fund, 130, 132
See also MSCI All-Country World Index;
S&P 500
index (passive) strategy, 55–6, 73–6
inflation, 18–19, 22, 24–7, 33–5, 53, 60, 64,
187–9
initial public offering (IPO), 136
Inside the Investor's Brain (Richard
Peterson), 194
instant gratification, 144–8
Intel, 79
Intelligent Investor, The (Graham), 95
investing hierarchy, 183–6
investment strategies
and consistency, 91–5
and holding periods, 192
index (passive) strategy, 55–6, 73–6
and momentum, 83, 85, 108, 113–15,
117–18, 184–5, 191–3
and perseverance, 91–4, 124
and quality over junk, 191
Sector Bargains strategy, 77, 80–4, 86–9,
111, 137
Sector Leaders strategy, 77–83, 86, 137
Sector Stalwarts strategy, 83–5
Sector Steadies strategy, 83–4
Sector Stewards strategy, 83–4, 101
Sector Winners strategy, 83–4, 113
smart strategies, 184–6
and stakeholder yield, 84, 102, 107–8,
116, 119, 184–5, 192–3
value investing, 81–2, 95, 110–11, 113
See also Millennial Money strategy
Ireland, 26–7
Italy, 26–7, 36, 47, 60, 173

James, Bill, 80
Japan, 26–7, 36, 57–60, 63, 82, 176
Johnson, Lyndon, 38
Johnson & Johnson, 78, 111

Kahneman, Daniel, 94, 165, 167
karma, 31–4, 40, 42, 48, 51
Kidd, Celeste, 147

Lefèvre, Edwin, 194
Legg Mason Opportunity Fund, 70–1
Legg Mason Value Trust, 70
Lewis, Michael, 80

life expectancy, 37, 48
Lincoln, Abraham, 20, 161
Livermore, Jesse, 194

Madden curse, 79
Mandelbrot, Benoît B., 194
market. *See* stock market
market bubbles, 29, 59, 129–30, 133, 156,
173, 175–9
Marsh, Paul, 66
McClure, Samuel, 147
Medicare, 20, 37–8, 40–2, 46–7, 50
Microsoft, 79
millennial generation
and concerns for retirement, 2–3, 14
defined, 13
demographics of, 13, 38
and index funds, 74
and portfolio allocation, 14, 24, 182
and risk, 2–4, 13–14, 137, 151–3, 167, 182
and taxes, 36, 38, 43, 195
Millennial Money strategy
and checklist approach, 97–8, 116, 118–20
and consistency, 94–5
costs of, 121–3
and earnings, 104–8, 117
investing hierarchy for, 183–5
and momentum, 113–15, 117–18
and perseverance, 91–4, 124
and ranking approach, 116, 120
and return on investment, 103–4, 117
and risk, 151–5
and rules for picking stocks, 95–120
and shareholder-friendly practices,
98–103, 116
using the, 120–1
and value, 108–12
Miller, Bill, 70
Mind of the Market, The (Shermer), 166
Minnesota twins study, 125–8
(mis)Behavior of Markets, The (Mandelbrot),
194
Mischel, Walter, 145–6
momentum, 83, 85, 108, 113–15, 117–18,
184–5, 191–3
Moneyball (Lewis), 80
Monsanto Company, 78
MSCI All Country World Index, 28, 65, 67,
72–3, 94, 130, 183
mutual funds, 67, 70–1, 73–5, 82, 86–7, 94,
130–1, 156, 160, 182–3, 193

NASDAQ, 176–7
Nash, J. Madeline, 156

Nelson, Willie, 113
Netherlands, 26–7, 63
New Zealand, 26–7
Newton, Isaac, 83
Nikkei, 57–9, 176–7
Nixon, Richard, 20–1, 24, 27, 60, 187–8
Norway, 26–7

O'Shaughnessy, James, 194
O'Shaughnessy Asset Management, 193
Oakland A's, 80–1
Oceanstone Fund, 130
Odean, Terrance, 137–8
one-year pledge, 92–3
overconfidence, 138, 175–9

Palmeri, Holly, 147
pattern-detection errors, 155–7, 166–7
perseverance, 91–4, 124
Personal Capital, 190, 195
Petajisto, Antti, 86–7
Peterson, Richard, 194
Pfizer, 66
pillar dollar, 8
plan sponsors, 159–60
Plus Ultra (Spain's national motto), 8
portfolio allocation, 14, 61–2, 132–3, 140,
    193, 195
portfolio patriotism, 61–2
Portfolio123, 121, 190
price-to-cash flow ratio, 112, 191
price-to-earnings (P/E) ratio, 95, 121, 172–3,
    178, 185, 187, 191
price-to-sales ratio, 112, 191
Procter & Gamble, 78
profit. *See* earnings
Pronovost, Peter, 95, 124

Quantitative Value (Gray), 190

ranking approach to picking stocks, 116, 120
real returns, 18–19, 22, 25–6, 29, 60, 71,
    149–50, 187
recession of 2007–2009, 62, 69
reckless acquirers, 99–100
Reminiscences of a Stock Operator
    (Lefèvre), 194
Research Affiliates, 193
retirement
    and baby boomers, 37–8, 43, 45–7, 50,
        110, 182
    and fertility rates, 36–7
    and life expectancy, 37
    millennials' concerns for, 2–3, 14

postponed, 36
    and Social Security, 37–8, 40–2, 44–8, 50
retirement plans, 28
    401(k), 33, 140–1, 183, 195
    automatic contributions to, 34, 51, 195
    and compounding, 7, 33–4
    investing hierarchy for, 183–6
    and smart indexes, 85, 183–6
return on invested capital (ROIC), 103–4,
    117–19
Rising Sun (Crichton), 57–8
risk
    career, 157–9
    defined, 3–4, 154
    and global investments, 54, 61, 65–7
    and heroes, 7–8
    and millennial generation, 2–4, 13–14,
        137, 151–3, 167, 182
    and Millennial Money strategy, 151–5
    redefined, 148–51
    of stocks, 28–9, 137, 148–54, 170, 182
Roosevelt, Franklin, 21, 38
Russell, Frank, 82
Russell 1000 Value, 82
Russell 3000 Value, 82

S&P 500, 62, 94, 96–7, 99–101
    and buy-and-hold return, 129–30, 132
    defined, 28, 72
    and fees, 74–5, 122–3
    and Schiller P/E ratio, 172
    and sector leaders, 78
    strategies for outperformance of, 70, 76–7,
        83–5, 96
    and technology bubble, 59
    Vanguard fund, 130, 132
Sapolsky, Robert, 171, 174
savings accounts, 12, 18, 24–6
savings rate, 2, 40–1, 49–50
Schauss, Alexander, 135
Schiller, Robert, 172
Sector Bargains strategy, 77, 80–4, 86–9,
    111, 137
Sector Leaders strategy, 77–83, 86, 137
Sector Stalwarts strategy, 83–5
Sector Steadies strategy, 83–4
Sector Stewards strategy, 83–4, 101
Sector Winners strategy, 83–4, 113
Segal, Nancy, 126
Seinfeld, Jerry, 93, 119, 124
shareholder stewards, 101–2
shareholder yield. *See* stakeholder yield
Shermer, Michael, 166
Shiv, Baba, 167–8

Siegel, Stephan, 127
smart indexes, 71, 80–3, 85, 88–9, 91, 116, 123, 141, 183, 193
smart strategies, 184–6
Social Security, 37–8, 40–2, 44–8, 50
South Africa, 26–7
South Korea, 63–4
Spain, 8, 26–7
Sports Illustrated curse, 79
stakeholder yield, 84, 102, 107–8, 116, 119, 184–5, 192–3
Staunton, Mike, 66
stock market
  adaptability of, 49–50
  bear, 130, 133, 148, 151, 167, 172–3
  bubbles, 29, 59, 129–30, 133, 156, 173, 175–9
  bull, 58, 133, 148, 156, 170, 172, 179
  competitiveness of, 196
  crashes, 3, 24, 26, 29, 35, 56, 69, 84, 129, 133, 156, 176, 182, 187
  global, 3, 7–8, 12–14, 47, 51, 55, 57–67, 72–4, 89, 141, 187, 195
  and greed, 175–9
  and momentum, 191–2
  resources on, 193–4
stock picking, 88–9, 91–5
  avoiding, 186
  rules for, 95–120
stocks and risk, 28–9, 137, 148–54, 170, 182
strategy, 91–2. *See also* investment strategies
Sweden, 26–7, 63, 127, 159
Switzerland, 26–7, 63

Templeton, John, 109–11, 179
The Can Kicks Back, 43
Thinking, Fast and Slow (Kahneman), 167
Treasury bills (T-bills), 25–8, 149–51

Triumph of the Optimists (Dimson, Marsh, and Staunton), 66
Truman, Harry, 175
Turnkey Analyst, 190
Tversky, Amos, 165, 167
twins. *See* Minnesota twins study
tyranny of compounding costs, 123
Tyson, Mike, 125

United Kingdom, 26–7, 62–3, 159, 172
US Federal Reserve, 22

valuation, 108–17, 171–3, 185, 191
value, 18–22, 24–7, 101–2, 108–13, 115–17, 183–6, 191, 193–4
value investing, 81–2, 95, 110–11, 113
Vanguard S&P 500 index fund, 130, 132

Wahal, Sunil, 159–60
wealth inequality, 34–5, 42
WealthFront, 190–1, 195
Welch, Ivo, 156
Wells Fargo, 78
What Makes Your Brain Happy and Why You Should Do the Opposite (DiSalvo), 134
What Works on Wall Street (O'Shaughnessy), 194
Wisdom Tree, 193
World War I, 60
World War II, 20, 40, 43, 60, 110
World War II generation, 13–14

Yahoo Finance, 121
Your Money & Your Brain (Zweig), 155

Zimbardo, Philip, 128
Zweig, Jason, 155